Revised
Edition

BUILDING
A STRIP CANOE

Gil Gilpatrick

DeLORME
PUBLISHING COMPANY

Dedication

To all my students, past and present, undergraduate and adult, who have built canoes in my shop, and have suffered through my many experiments and changes.

Acknowledgement

I would again like to express my thanks to the staff, administration, and board of directors of Maine School Administrative District #54 in Skowhegan, Maine, who have given such wholehearted support to me and my program, of which canoe building is a part. Without this enthusiastic and far-sighted support, this book would not have been possible.

Table of Contents

Introduction

One of the hardest things for a writer to face is the fact that what is written today may not be so tomorrow, or a year from now. Five years ago, as I was writing the original *Building a Strip Canoe,* I finished the book with an epilogue called "Looking Ahead" in which I acknowledged that there probably would be changes in the future. But, I remember thinking then, deep down, that I couldn't see how, after ten years of building strip canoes, I could discover any ideas that I had not already tried. You hold in your hands the proof of how wrong that kind of thinking can be.

Because of the high interest in canoe building in my area of Maine, I have found myself in a very unique situation that allows me to try out every new method or product that comes along, every new design or idea that I can dream up. Strip-canoe building is part of the course I teach at the Skowhegan Regional Vocational Center, and my students and I build about eight to ten canoes per year in that program. Also, I teach an evening adult course in canoe building, and we build six to ten canoes per year. They all add up — 15 to 20 canoes per year for the past five years comes to 75 to 100 canoes! Before that, I figure that I had seen the building of about 125 strip canoes; so by now I have been directly involved with the construction of well over 200 canoes.

The proof of the pudding is in the eating, they say, and I am fortunate enough to spend a good amount of time using my canoes. During the summer months I operate a guiding business on Maine's wilderness rivers. On these trips I always use a 20 ′ strip canoe, and I provide these craft for my guests, too, if they have at least a little canoeing experience. This way, each summer I can evaluate the previous winter's work — that is, any new curve in design or construction that affects the quality of the finished canoe.

One of the greatest sources of satisfaction to me has been the response to *Building a Strip Canoe,* the letters and calls I have received from successful canoe builders or from folks who are about to build a canoe. I can truthfully say that I never received a negative comment, but sometimes there was a question — and this meant that I had probably left out some things that should have been covered in the book. I have made sure to answer all of those questions in this completely revised edition, along with adding updated instructions on using the latest materials.

No one ever complains about the lack of safety instruction until an accident happens or a health problem develops. I never heard from any reader in this regard, although one book reviewer did mention it. Recently, there has been a marked increase in safety awareness in industry and in the schools. Though in some cases caution gets carried to ridiculous extremes, this is a good trend, and I have supported it here by including a rather lengthy chapter on health and safety precautions in canoe building that the lay person would not ordinarily be familiar with. I hope you take the time to read the material that is new to you.

New Designs

Less than a year after the original *Building a Strip Canoe* was published, I got my hands on two authentic E. M. White canoes, an 18½-footer and a 20-footer. Having long admired the design, I quickly lifted patterns from them, and within a year they became the most popular canoes in my programs. They were so well liked, and so beautiful, that already I regretted that I had been unable to include this design in the book. Happily, with this book, that situation is now remedied. The other new designs included here are the square-sterned Grand Laker and a solo canoe, the Wabnaki.

The Grand Laker is intended to fill the needs of fishermen, and others, who want a large canoe, but who are not all that interested in paddling. Many readers have asked about square-sterned canoes. Of course, any of the canoes in this book could be made as a square-stern, simply by making the last station permanent. The Grand Laker, though, is designed from stem to stern for use with an outboard motor.

As for the Wabnaki, in it I combined my own ideas and the features of a lot of canoe designs that I like. I don't really claim to have designed the Wabnaki, but I can't seem to blame anyone else, either. The name came to mind as a result of a lot of research I did on the Wabnaki (Abnaki) Indians for my novel, *Allagash*.[1] The process of researching and writing gave me a deep respect for these people, and the solo canoe I had set out to make somehow reminded me of them; so the name just seemed natural.

Construction and Materials

Nothing major has changed in the methods I use to bring the hull to the point of fiberglassing. Still, some little tricks have been learned, and each one that has proven itself has been included here. These shortcuts do not seriously alter the finished product, but only make construction a little easier. It is at the fiberglassing stage that I've discovered techniques that *do* have an effect on the finished product, and all for the better.

You will read of my trials and tribulations with epoxy resins in the chapter on fiberglassing, so just let me say here that as sad as those first attempts were, the canoes they produced showed me the need to perfect the technique of using epoxy resins. I was not really proud of that first epoxy canoe I took on the Allagash River that summer, although we had managed to make it presentable by extensive sanding. Still, a good craftsman could see the

flaws. However, by season's end I knew I had a good canoe; and the following fall, I found the Gougeon Brothers and WEST SYSTEM* brand epoxy. I was on my way.

Through the past few years I have found that I need to make heavier gunwales than those described in the original book. This does not make the narrower gunwales wrong, but thicker ones are used on the canoes we turn out now. Other than that, the woodwork is the same.

I have expanded the seat-making into a chapter of its own because of the interest my students at Skowhegan have shown in this important part of the canoe. As simple as the wooden frame looks at first glance, they found that to make strong, long-lasting seats requires careful craftsmanship and a little knowledge of wood joinery. I've provided instructions on caning to make the book complete.

The reason I have never before written about making canoe paddles is that I had not yet made a paddle I felt was worth writing about. I was not interested in just making a paddle to save money; I wanted one that was better than any I could buy. Lest I sound too conceited, I will qualify myself and say that the paddle in this book is the best *I* have used for *my* purposes. (Time will tell how many of my readers agree with me!)

Of all the communication I have had from readers of the original *Building a Strip Canoe,* the most frequent question asked has been, "Where do I find -----?" The word in that blank was usually wood, either cedar or ash. I have tried to answer this question in Appendix I with a lengthy list of suppliers — not just for wood, but for any materials that might be hard to find. I would like to stress that you should exhaust every possible local source, especially for lumber, before ordering from very far away. The woods I use are abundant in my area (though high-quality lumber is still at a premium), so explore the possibility of substituting a wood from your own area that may serve just as well.

Good luck with your canoe! I hope we meet on a river some day. Our canoes will be our introduction.

[1]Gil Gilpatrick, *Allagash: The Story of Maine's Legendary Wilderness Waterway* (Freeport, Maine: DeLorme Publishing Co., 1983).

*Trademark of Gougeon Brothers, Inc., U.S.A.

Safety

It is difficult to know how far to go in warning people about safety. To an experienced craftsperson, much of what can be said will be superfluous. On the other hand, a person who has little or no experience may well appreciate and benefit from advice. In a vocational shop situation we assume the student has no experience or knowledge and move on from there, even though we know, in most cases, that what we are presenting is not new to the student. Thorough instruction in the use and safety of tools is given, followed by safety testing in all power tools. Only then can the student proceed to the instructive work he has signed up for.

It would seem that most people considering the construction of a project as large as a canoe would have a working knowledge of woodworking tools and some appreciation of the dangers involved in their use. With this in mind, I have limited the scope of this chapter to basically three materials with which the usual craftsperson, amateur or professional, would not be so likely to have experience — resins, solvents, and wood dust. For what follows, except for the section on polyester resins, I am indebted to the folks at Gougeon Brothers, Inc., who have allowed me to make extensive use of the chapter on safety from their book.[1] The materials they sell are what I use and recommend. Their instructions are appropriate, well researched, and presented in easy-to-understand language.

Toxicity of Epoxy Resins

Epoxy resins and particularly hardeners have long had a reputation as skin sensitizers. Fortunately, the Gougeons have been able to minimize this problem by carefully selecting ingredients for WEST SYSTEM resins which maintain the necessary physical properties with the lowest possible toxicity. They and other builders have worked on a daily basis with WEST SYSTEM resins and hardeners without any harmful effects, but they have also taken precautions to minimize their actual skin contact with the materials. I must point out that there is a great variety of epoxy resins on the market, and each resin may have its own set of potential health hazards. The following discussion is specifically limited to WEST SYSTEM epoxy resins.

The main adverse effect of WEST SYSTEM resins on some individuals is a skin rash much like poison ivy. In most cases, this rash develops after the user has had repeated contact with the resins and hardeners over a long period of time. It depends largely on three factors: the degree of contact with the material, individual body chemistry, and state of health. Individuals who are "atopic" — that is, prone to allergies, hay fever, or asthmatic reactions — are more likely to become sensitized. For reasons not yet entirely clear, sensitivity to epoxy resins seems to be more often experienced by individuals with light complexions; conversely, individuals with dark complexions have proven less sensitive. General state of health seems to affect sensitivity, in that if you are suffering from fatigue, a viral infection, a cold, or a sore throat, your body is much more likely to become sensitized. While there may be little that you can do to control your sensitivity to WEST SYSTEM resins, there are steps you can take to minimize skin contact and keep your body in good health.

WEST SYSTEM 105 resin by itself rarely causes skin sensitization. The 205 and 206 hardeners,

[1]Gougeon Brothers, *The Gougeon Brothers on Boat Construction*, 3rd ed. (Bay City, Michigan, 1982), pp. 47-53, 79-85, 91-94.

however, are considered serious irritants and sensitizers, and the manufacturer advises that you take extreme precautions to prevent any direct skin contact with them. Once the 205 or 206 hardeners are diluted through mixture in a 1:5 ratio with the 105 resin, their toxic potential is greatly reduced. Nonetheless, you should still handle the resulting mixture with adequate precautions.

Sensitization results when the body will no longer tolerate any skin contact with a particular chemical. It then produces an antigen that causes a rash to break out in the areas of contact, usually on the hands, arms, or face. Once you have become sensitive to a given chemical, you may remain sensitive for life. Therefore, if you do become sensitized, you will have to take extraordinarily good precautions in the future; any contact whatsoever with the chemicals will usually bring back the old symptoms.

It makes good sense simply to eliminate the risk of sensitization. The Gougeons have found that it is not difficult to prevent skin contact from occurring in normal boatbuilding situations, and they recommend the following basic safeguards:

(1) As a minimum protection, use a barrier skin cream on any areas of the skin that are likely to come in contact with resin. These might include the forearms and face, as well as the hands. The cream quickly dries to provide an excellent protective coating.

(2) To provide your hands with additional protection, you should use thin, surgical-type plastic gloves. These are inexpensive enough so that you can dispose of them after use. Plastic gloves are far superior to skin cream when you are doing long bonding operations because handling a lot of stock might cause you to wear through the cream. The gloves also simplify cleanup. Because resin cures much more quickly when it is close to your warm skin than it does normally on a joint or wood surface, resin on your hands may be in an advanced state of cure after only 45 minutes and become very difficult to wash off. However, this is no problem if you are wearing the gloves, which you can just peel off and dispose of when the job is done. If you are involved in particularly long bonding operations, you can neutralize resin on the gloves before it cures by using an industrial hand cleanser.

(3) DON'T USE SOLVENTS FOR REMOVING WEST SYSTEM resins from the skin *except as a last resort*. Solvents themselves are skin sensitizers and their use will add to skin problems. Also, many solvents, such as acetone, have a high evaporation rate and can produce extreme drying of the skin by removing the natural protective oils. Dry skin is much more likely than normal healthy skin to become sensitized to irritants.

(4) When performing particularly messy operations, wear disposable, low-cost shop aprons or old throwaway clothes to protect your clothes as well as yourself. Resin can easily soak through clothes, come in contact with your skin, and bond the clothing to the skin when it cures. If you spill resin on your clothes, remove them *immediately* and use a solvent to clean the resin from the clothing. Otherwise, when it cures it will cause hard spots that are likely to break and tear and ruin the clothing.

(5) Be extremely careful when sanding partially cured WEST SYSTEM resins. When the 105 resin and 205 or 206 hardeners have cured properly, they are nontoxic. However, a full cure takes anywhere from four to seven days, depending on environmental conditions, and the resin-hardener mixture retains some of its toxicity until cured. This is of little concern except when you sand the material in its "green," or partially cured, state. The dust from this "green" material can cause some problems with those individuals who are either already sensitized or have particularly sensitive body chemistry. The toxic effect seems to be maximized if the dust settles on skin that is already wet with perspiration. This dust could also possibly cause an asthma-like reaction in previously sensitized individuals who inhale it. Up to this point, however, there are no known cases of anyone suffering from this reaction.

(6) ENSURE ADEQUATE VENTILATION. Fumes and vapors given off by various products are another safety concern. WEST SYSTEM 105 resin itself produces a negligible fume level which is not considered dangerous. The 205 and 206 hardeners do give off fumes, although they are slight and not likely to cause any problem unless you use the hardeners in a confined area with no ventilation. The hardener vapors are minimized considerably when the hardener is mixed in its proper ratio with the 105 resin. The resulting mixture has a very low fume level as long as you use it in a well-ventilated building. In close quarters, such as the interior of a boat, or when you are working near the stem on the inside of your canoe, you should make provisions for vigorous air cir-

culation to keep the fume level down to a minimum, or at least make a conscious effort to keep your head above the gunwale where there is fresh air. Although it might be possible, there are no known cases of anyone who has become sensitized to the resin through contact with the fumes only. However, some people who have already become sensitized to the resin through skin contact may suffer an adverse reaction when exposed to the fumes alone. Generally, the reaction is a skin rash like that caused by actual contact, but asthma-like constriction of the bronchial air passages may also develop, causing shortness of breath.

(7) If you develop a skin rash while working with WEST SYSTEM resins, the best course of action is to stop working with the product until the rash goes away completely (usually three or four days). When you go back to work with the product, improve your safety precautions and aim to prevent any skin contact whatsoever with the resins. I would think a person would have to be supersensitive to the product to have a problem when building just one canoe, or even one or two every year.

(8) Take particular care to protect your eyes from contact with WEST SYSTEM 205 or 206 hardeners. If contact should occur, immediately flush your eyes with liberal amounts of water under low pressure for a period of 15 minutes; if there is still discomfort, seek medical attention immediately.

Solvents

Because of the dangers involved in a school shop situation, I have almost completely eliminated the use of solvents. Other than a little paint thinner and a very little WEST SYSTEM #850 cleaning solvent, I use none. I clean up the roller frames by wiping them off, using no solvent. I clean up the squeegees by flexing them when the resin has hardened, then peeling it off. I clean up the roller trays by flexing them and popping out the hardened resin. In short, I keep the solvent around in case I ever need it, but the need never seems to arise. The point is, you can complete your canoe with no solvents, and eliminate their danger. I recommend you do this. But, if you *do* plan to use them, read on.

Fume Level Hazards: Solvents present a safety problem. They are indispensable to the average boatbuilder, but they can also be very hazardous. In recent years, both government and industry have taken an increasingly critical look at a wide variety of commonly used solvents. Some of these

once-common solvents, such as carbon tetrachloride, have been found to be so dangerous that they have been eliminated for the most part from common usage. Other solvents are beginning to be labeled as highly dangerous and are under the scrutiny of the Occupational Safety and Health Administration (OSHA).

One health problem associated with solvents is the drying effect that solvent fumes have on the air passageways. This tendency is known to interfere with the natural ability of the lungs to cleanse themselves of impurities. (More on this in the section on dust.)

Another major concern is the general anesthetic effect of breathing high concentrations of solvent vapors. For example, the solvent chloroform was used as an anesthetic for many years. If concentrations of solvent fumes become high enough, a person can be anesthetized to varying degrees and suffer effects such as dizziness, nausea, headaches, and, in the extreme, loss of consciousness. These anesthetic effects may impair the sound judgment of a worker and thus jeopardize his safety. Another danger to some people could be an asthmatic reaction resulting in the onset of bronchial spasms caused by a sensitivity to a particular vapor.

Some, but not all, solvents have been suspected to be potentially carcinogenic. The government, through OSHA, has established permissible exposure levels (PEL) for nearly all solvents. Each value is a time-weighted average for an eight-hour day and provides acceptable levels of exposure in the workplace. Research in toxicology laboratories of solvent manufacturers has also provided data identifying odor threshold concentrations as well as fume levels that can cause the onset of anesthetic effects.

I have not included here the tables of established PEL because they are intended primarily for industrial use where workers are exposed on a daily basis. However, the importance of possible toxic effects should not be minimized for the home canoe-building operation, and if you use them, take care. I have been dealing with various solvents and chemicals in my canoe building for over 15 years now without incident, except one which I will discuss under the section on polyester resins. A liberal dose of good old common sense in providing a well-ventilated area, and listening attentively when your body (in this case your nose) tries to tell you something, are the most important things you can do to ensure your continued good health when dealing with solvents.

Fire Hazards: It is important to realize that probably the greatest hazard of solvents to both life and property is fire. Most solvents are extremely flammable and are frequent causes of industrial fires. It is a common mistake to think only of straight solvent as a fire risk; in fact, it is usually a can of paint or other formulated product containing a high percentage of solvent thinner that is the culprit. Smoking around solvents should absolutely not be allowed.

The table below lists the comparative flash points and lower explosive limits for some common boatbuilding solvents.

Solvent	Flash Point	%LEL
Acetone	0° F	2.1
Methylene chloride	NF	---
Perchloroethylene	NF	---
Methyl ethyl ketone	30° F	1.8
Toluene	40° F	1.3
Turpentine	93° F	0.8
Xylene	63° F	1.1

Flash Point = The lowest temperature at which flammable vapor is given off by a liquid in a test vessel in sufficient concentration to be ignited in air when exposed momentarily to a source of ignition.

LEL = Lower explosive limit. This is the volume percentage of the vaporized solvent that makes an explosive mixture in air.

NF = Nonflammable. The lower the flash point, the more hazardous the liquid. Of the solvents listed above, methylene chloride and perchloroethylene are nonflammable and have no explosive concentration level. The remainder of the solvents are all flammable, with acetone being the most hazardous in this regard.

In a typical boatbuilding operation, where any of these solvents is used for occasional cleanup, there is little likelihood that fume level concentrations will even reach anesthetic levels, let alone the much higher explosive concentrations. The danger increases as the amount of solvent used in a given time period increases, assuming there is little or no ventilation. In an enclosed hull, washing the entire inside surface with a solvent that has a high evaporation rate, such as acetone, could raise fume levels to a point where explosion is a real possibility. The situation in which an explosion is more likely to occur is during spray-painting, where solvent fumes are concentrated in a confined area without ventilation. As temperatures increase, the concentrations required for explosion to occur are significantly lower. The addition of wood dust also lowers the concentration of solvent fumes needed to cause an explosion. The highest danger of explosion is when there is a mixture of dust and fumes, especially during the hot summer months.

Wood dust by itself also has a dangerous explosion potential. For a wood such as spruce, a concentration of 35 grams per cubic meter (.035 ounces per cubic foot) is sufficient to cause an explosion. Obviously, one worker involved in a hand-sanding operation would not generate enough dust to worry about, but several workers operating power-sanding equipment could. Open flames are not necessary to set the explosion off; static electricity can provide the spark.

WEST SYSTEM solvent is a blend of methylene chloride, perchloroethylene, and dipropylene glycol methyl ether. This solvent is nonflammable and has a reduced evaporation rate from that of methylene chloride. Methylene chloride has so little odor that fume concentrations could exceed the recommended threshold limit value (200 ppm) before the average individual is able to detect the odor. Therefore, the manufacturer has added perchloroethylene with an odor threshold of 50 ppm so that you can smell the fume concentrations before they reach the recommended threshold limit value. Based on the information that the Gougeons have gathered to date concerning solvents, they feel that this combination of ingredients gives the safest possible solvent that meets cleanup requirements. The fact that WEST SYSTEM solvent has no flash point provides considerable peace of mind for them, their insurance company, and us.

Two final points are well worth knowing about WEST SYSTEM solvent and methylene chloride. Although they are nonflammable, introducing these solvents to high temperatures, such as fire, will result in a breakdown to more dangerous chemicals, including hydrogen chloride. Therefore, you should avoid using cutting torches or other burners directly on them. In addition, you should store these solvents away from an area where there is the possibility of fire. Finally, these solvents have negligible photochemical reactivity, and do not contribute to the formation of smog. Therefore, they are not regulated by the existing pollution-control regulations.

Dust

Almost by definition, a boatshop, or canoe shop, is usually a dusty place. Boatbuilders commonly coexist with high levels of dust that are by-products of the sawing and sanding involved in boat manufacture. For many years the Gougeons breathed a lot of dust in their own boatbuilding operations with no apparent problems. But, after hearing of lung problems (silicosis, asbestosis, byssinosis) that developed in other industries after long periods of exposure, they began to be concerned about possible long-range problems with their own situation. They studied the data available and consulted with several experts, including a well-known pulmonary (lung) specialist who had worked widely with industry on dust-related problems for many years, and the following are their findings:

> The world is full of dust, and normally our lungs deal successfully with a large volume of foreign particles each day through highly sophisticated, multi-stage defense mechanisms. The main mechanism is a system of fine hairs (cilia) that are found throughout the inner air passages. These fine hairs always exist in a moving sea of water and their main function is, by an undulating motion, to propel this mucous material ever upward toward the oral and nasal areas. This moist mucous covering of all the air passages attracts foreign material much like flypaper, and then moves it harmlessly up and out of the lung area.
>
> With this defense mechanism, the lungs are capable of withstanding incredible abuse, but there are limits. Smoking, dry air, and excessive dust all put extra demands on the lungs. We have all heard that smoking is bad because it is a cause of lung cancer, but it also heavily taxes the defense mechanisms of the lungs by adding impurities that must be removed. In addition, cigarette smoke is hot and dry, which contributes to another problem. Dry air dries out this mucous covering of the lungs' airways. This drying of the lung tissue seriously impedes the functioning of the cleansing mechanism, preventing lung tissue from properly dealing with all foreign matter, including disease-causing germs. The great increase in bronchial problems during the winter is a direct result of breathing extremely dry air. Relative humidity levels below 40% are harmful; a minimum of 60% is preferable.

It doesn't take a doctor to tell us that breathing concentrated amounts of dust is bad. Surprisingly enough, however, the doctor the Gougeons consulted was not nearly as concerned about high dust levels as he was about having very healthy lungs that were capable of dealing with high dust levels. It was his experience that breathing dust alone was rarely the cause of serious lung problems; most of his patients were also heavy smokers. He felt that if you smoked, breathed dry air, and inhaled a high amount of dust all at the same time, you were in for trouble. To avoid possible lung problems you can stop smoking (easier said than done), humidify your breathing air to at least 40%, and minimize the breathable dust that is produced in the boatshop. The following are suggestions to minimize dust:

(1) Set up a separate sanding area with its own exhaust fan. A temporary wall of polyethylene sheet plastic works well.

(2) Install dust collectors on your major dust-making tools (table saw, planer, power sander).

(3) Perform more operations with cutting tools (such as a hand plane) rather than abrading tools (such as sandpaper), which make more dust.

(4) Wet-sand rather than dry-sand whenever possible.

(5) Purchase a comfortable and effective dust mask, make sure that it fits correctly, and wear it whenever dust levels are high in the shop. In the Gougeons' own shop, they utilize double-cartridge face masks which can be modified simply by changing cartridges to provide protection against either dust or solvents. Very simple, effective, and cheap face masks are available for dust alone. One of the better types is the simple, disposable pressed-cloth mask manufactured by 3M.

Dust can be a serious problem to the large shop. In fact, it was necessary for us to install a dust-collection system in my school shop, where several canoes are often under construction at any one time. But, the problem is minimal for the home canoe-builder. Certain woods are more likely to cause problems than others, but to list them here is a poor use of space because the part-time builder would never become exposed to enough dust to cause problems. In my shop we use the pressed-cloth masks mentioned above whenever dust levels are high. Probably of greater interest to the canoe-builder is the dust produced from sanding products other than wood, namely the resins and fiberglass used on the canoe. The following two paragraphs deal with this.

There are, of course, many other types of dust in the boatshop. I have already referred to the dust that can be generated from sanding cured WEST SYSTEM resins. Basically, this dust is inert and cannot give off any toxic elements that would be harmful. In addition, the shape and size of the dust granule is not unusual and does not present any undue problem for the lungs to expel. There are other WEST SYSTEM ingredients that are in powder or fiber form that are added to the WEST SYSTEM resin. None of these ingredients present any toxic potential and they are not unusually hazardous to breathe in small concentrations, with the possible exception of the 403 Microfibers. This product is basically cotton fibers which, when breathed in large quantities over a long period of time, can cause a lung disease called byssinosis. Typically, the only exposure to the product in its fiber form is when you mix it in with the resin. If properly done, the mixing process does not release many fibers into the air, and it is not thought that this limited exposure is of great concern. Sanding a cured 403 mixture produces a dust composed of a cured resin-fiber matrix; the fibers are tightly locked up within the resin matrix and are no longer harmful.

Not all dust problems manifest themselves in the lungs. Several years ago, before the dust collection system was installed in my shop, I experienced what seemed to be an eye infection. It was serious and persistent enough that I went to my eye doctor. He diagnosed it as an allergic reaction of unknown origin. But, he observed that I "reeked of wood dust" (I went there directly from my shop), and that it was the probable cause. The condition went away with no more treatment than some drops to relieve the discomfort, and it has not returned. The two most common woods we use are white cedar and white ash, so one of them is the culprit, probably the cedar. Bear in mind, though, that I work in this environment five days a week for almost ten months of the year. The canoe-builder making a canoe or two at home should experience nothing more serious than an occasional sneeze.

Polyester Resins

The subject of polyester resins is being discussed here, rather than with the epoxy resins, in order to maintain the continuity of the safety chapter from the Gougeons' book. My forté is definitely not chemistry, so this section is based on my years of practical use of the resins, advice from professional users of the chemicals, and information obtained from publications, mainly of the National Institute for Occupational Safety and Health (NIOSH). Early on in this chapter the Gougeons stated that their discussion was limited to WEST SYSTEM epoxy resins; that other brands may have their own characteristics. So, too, has my experience been limited to certain brands of resins, and others may have characteristics with which I am unfamiliar. The point of all this is that the user *must* read and follow the manufacturer's instructions for the sake of safety as well as for satisfactory results.

From what I have been able to determine in my reading, the bad guy in polyester resin is not the resin itself (which the safety literature almost ignores) but the catalyst that must be added just before use. The most common of the catalysts, and

the only one I have had experience with, is methyl ethyl ketone peroxide. Usually identified simply as MEK peroxide, it is supplied along with the resin in a small plastic bottle. It is fortunate that the canoe-builder will require only small quantities of this material, because the stuff has the potential of being a real troublemaker. You should remember that, although in use the MEK peroxide is greatly diluted by the resin, you are spreading it over a large area and so exposing yourself to any possible harmful effects. The following are the safe-handling rules established by NIOSH. They were originally presented for industrial use; I have modified them for the home user.

• Never mix peroxides directly with accelerators or promoters. A violent explosion can result. (You should not have to worry about this, as the accelerators and promoters should already have been added to your resin. However, don't add the stuff to *anything* except that for which it is intended.)

• Keep all work areas, tools, and containers clean. Avoid mixing contaminated peroxides with any other substance.

• Weigh (or measure) in a special room or area apart from any activity. Never use a storage area containing other peroxides. The mixing area should be well ventilated and have a means of extinguishing chemical fires.

• While using resin containing peroxide, or handling the peroxide, have a means available for washing out the eyes. (The rule in industry, or school shops, is to wash the eyes for 15 minutes with water under low pressure. If there is pain after this, seek medical attention.)

• Adding peroxides to hot resins is dangerous. (I can't see why you'd want to do that.)

• Never dilute peroxide solutions. Using the wrong solvent or a contaminated solvent can cause a violent reaction. (This goes right back to the first rule.)

• Mixing and dispensing containers should be polyethylene, Teflon, glass, or stainless steel (304 or 316). (Brass, copper, zinc, galvanized finishes, and some steels and aluminum alloys are corroded by peroxides, and this corrosion can trigger a peroxide fire or explosion. Paper containers and wooden stirrers are good for one-time use.)

• Never return excess peroxides to storage containers. Don't use glass for storage as any pressure buildup can shatter the container.

• Keep all containers tightly closed to prevent contamination.

• Use an electrical ground or bonding strap with any processing equipment. (You will not be likely to have processing equipment, but be aware of the danger of static spark.)

• Don't use acetone to dilute peroxide solutions or to clean containers or tools. Acetone reacts with some peroxides to form explosive compounds. (Follow the manufacturer's directions on cleanup if you need any; usually you can use throwaway tools and avoid the need for cleaning solvents.)

If these rules make the stuff seem scary, that is good. I once stated in writing a safety chapter for whitewater canoeing, that no one ever drowned on a portage. Being overcautious can't hurt! However, in fairness, and to relieve *some* of your apprehension, I should say that I have used polyester resins for years in my high school vocational shop, with 16- to 18-year-old students, without serious incident, making good old common sense the golden rule of the fiberglass room.

I have had one case of a person becoming anesthetized while using polyester resin. He was an elderly man in my adult canoe-building class. The work was being done in a large shop area with adequate ventilation. He fell onto the canoe being fiberglassed, but did not completely lose consciousness. He went to his knees, and we helped him outside to fresh air. Apparently he was sensitive to the fumes, as no one else was bothered, and for the remainder of the course we found other work for him to do.

I have had three or four incidents where students were sensitive to the resin (or catalyst). They broke out with a rash and had some itching for about a day. Only with one incident was the rash and discomfort bad enough that any school was missed. Since I have had hundreds of students over the years, I have to conclude that the chance of a person being sensitive to the material on first contact is slight. However, common sense dictates that one should provide adequate protection to ensure that none of the material touches the skin.

One student got some of the material into his eye. The recommended time at the eyewash station took care of it, with no other action being necessary. This incident took place before safety glasses were required full-time in my shop. While the glasses are not 100 percent insurance against the possibility of a splash, they do give excellent protection.

Once last incident comes to mind that I would like to relate before closing this very important chapter on safety. This happened to a man who built a canoe in his home basement. After the fiberglassing was over and the canoe was all but finished, the man (or his distraught wife) discovered that everything in their home freezer (also in the basement) had the taste of polyester resin. Some foods were more flavorful than others, but I believe they threw out most everything that was stored there. I am happy to report that the last I knew, the couple were still together.

In closing this chapter I would like to quote from the final paragraph of the Gougeons' safety chapter, which very well sums up theirs and mine:

> We hope that we have not scared you away with this candid discussion of what we feel are significant hazards. We feel that with foresight you can easily deal with them to produce safe working conditions. However, it is important to realize that reactions can be cumulative. If you are having a toxic reaction, it may not be from one cause, but from a combination of sensitivity to the resin, solvents, and wood dust. While you might not react to any one of these individually, their combined effect might be hazardous. The same is true with lung problems. A combination of smoking and inhaling wood dust and solvent fumes could produce breathing problems, while no one of these hazards by itself might be enough to cause the problem. Precaution, good health, and safe working conditions are the best way to avoid health risks.

The Canoe Models

The designs I have selected to be included in this book are those I have found the most popular in my canoe-building classes, or best suited for my own use. Four of them were in the original *Building a Strip Canoe*. The other four I have adopted since its publication. (No doubt, my preferences have influenced my students. Every teacher has to come to terms with this fact. All we can teach is what we know and believe in. When the student has learned this, then it is time for independent thinking on his part.)

To choose a design, you must first consider how you intend to use the canoe. Will it be used primarily on a lake, a flat river, or in whitewater? Will it be used for lengthy trips on wilderness waters or just for daily recreation? This is not to say that a canoe designed for one purpose cannot be used for another; if this were the case, everyone would need a backyard full of canoes! The canoe is a versatile craft, and one canoe can serve you well. But, if you know how your canoe is going to be used most of the time, why not take advantage of that knowledge and use a design that will meet your needs most of the time?

The major differences in canoe design are shown in Figure 1. A person with a moderate amount of experience could appreciate these variations as soon as he or she had the canoes in the water. However, the various subtle changes to these basic forms that are possible would take an expert to detect, and miles of practical use to appreciate.

Let's look at the major considerations in canoe design, how they have shaped my selections, and how they will affect you:

Flat Bottom versus Round Bottom: This is basically a question of stability and capacity versus speed. As I am not into racing, my canoes tend to be flat-bottomed or slightly rounded. The increased stability is appreciated by the novice in flat water and by everyone in whitewater. There is a term called "secondary stability" you may see used by some canoe writers when describing a round-bottomed canoe. The idea is that a round-bottomed canoe, while it may seem initially unstable in the water, will actually be more stable after being tipped beyond a certain point. I cannot fault the reasoning behind this, but have found the information of little practical use and hard to demonstrate satisfactorily on the water.

Keel or Not? The keel keeps the canoe running straight, and so helps a novice in flat water. Many people expect the keel to add stability to the canoe, but I don't think it does this to any significant degree. What gives the canoe stability is the flat or nearly flat bottom found on most canoes that have a keel. People unfamiliar with canoes are fond of saying a canoe is "tippy" (or not). This tippiness is the product of the canoe's profile, not the keel or lack of it. The keel affords some protection to the hull if you hit a rock. Yet the added stiffness to the hull is a questionable advantage. The keel is a nightmare in whitewater. It makes maneuvering difficult, and adds to the depth of the canoe, thus decreasing clearance and increasing the chance of becoming hung up on a rock.

Rocker: Canoes with rocker are generally recognized as river canoes. The upturned ends, in effect, give the canoe bottom a rounded shape which makes it easier to turn. Think how easily a round tub would spin and turn — this is the theory behind that rounded shape. I have provided the river canoes for my guests, and they have used them about equally in flat water and whitewater. They are perfectly satisfactory in flat water and a joy to

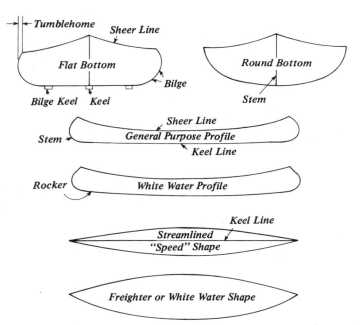

FIGURE 1 · Basic Canoe Shapes and Nomenclature

use in whitewater. Pick your canoe for what is important to you and for what it will be used for most of the time.

Height of Stem: This is a matter of personal preference and utility. The classic high stem with all its gracefulness and eye appeal probably evolved from Indian ceremonial designs or even from the idealistic eye of long-forgotten artists who took artistic license with their work. However these high stems came about, they are not too practical. Wind has too much surface to get hold of. Most modern canoe designs keep the stems low.

Streamlined or Freighter Shape? I think most canoes are a compromise in this department. There *are* racers that use the one extreme, and freighters that use the other. The extra width in the ends of the freighter or whitewater shape gives ''lift'' in whitewater; this is important when the canoe pitches down from one level to another. Of course, it means extra flotation for hauling freight or using a motor.

The shape of a canoe is a hard thing to communicate from one person to another. Specifications, length, width, depth, etc., tell something about a canoe, but are all but useless in comparing one with another. Two canoes with identical specifications could be very different in appearance and purpose. A skilled person can make a set of drawings that will show the true shape of a hull. The only problem is that it requires an almost equally skilled person to read the drawings! Lacking the skill to

make the drawings and assuming that most of you lack the skill to read them, I have to rely on words and photos to help you make your choice. I have offered eight models, and there are several easy variations of these. If none of them pleases you, read on to the chapter on designs — you can make your own, or copy or adapt someone else's.

The E. M. White Designs

Specifications:	18' Guide	20' Guide
Length	18' 6"	20'0"
Width	34½"	41"
Depth	12"	13"
Height of stems	23"	24"
Approximate weight	75 lbs	90 lbs

''Mr. White, I made a mistake.''
''Did you learn anything from it?''
''Sure did.''
''Well then, it was no mistake.''

This conversation between the founder of the E. M. White Canoe Company and one of his young employees sums up the employee-employer relationship that existed, and gives us some insight as to the kind of man he was.

E. M. White was born and brought up on the Penobscot River in Maine and learned to love the water at an early age. His father was an expert paddle- and oar-maker (bateau oars were his specialty), and the younger White built his first canoe in his father's shop in the late 1880s. Someone bought it on its maiden voyage, and the White Canoe Company was launched.

''Someone wanted that canoe more than I did, so I sold it, built another, and another, and I've been at it ever since.''

White took the lines for his canoe from those of the Indian canoes that had been moving up and down Penobscot waters for countless centuries. It is interesting that the wood-and-canvas canoe that made the White name famous came into being not because it was considered better at the time, but because the large canoe birches were becoming harder and harder to find. The white man used too many. More plentiful materials had to be found.

Just how closely the White design follows the old Indian designs is hard to determine. Never having seen more than a token number of old birchbark canoes, I cannot say firsthand. I have studied

The big 20′ White Guide and I swap roles going around Allagash Falls on the Allagash River.

photos of bark canoes, and it becomes a case of personal interpretation. Since you can only see one view from a photograph, you have to imagine the rest. I have taken it on faith that it is true, based on the fact that company records and written accounts of people who should have known seem to bear it out. I have seen a photograph of several guides in their canoes, probably taken at Moosehead Lake, Maine, in the very early 1900s. The wood-canvas canoes in the photo are unquestionably Whites. Some of the guides were standing in birch canoes

that did bear a strong resemblance to their more modern counterparts.

The two White designs I have presented in this book are called "Guide" models, though I am not sure that designation is entirely correct. Not that guides didn't use that design, but early brochures loaned to me by the company indicate that a canoe was designated "Guide Model" not because it was a special design for the exclusive use of those woodsmen, but because it was: "planned throughout for hunting and fishing . . . no money put into

The sleek and graceful 18′ White Guide is being loaded for the day's travel.

15

The 16' White Water is a good sporting canoe for one or two people. It performs beautifully in the rapids.

ornamenting . . . carried in stock painted drab or slate-color only." In other words, it was a plain canoe built for work, not for show. Your strip-built White design will please both the artist and craftsman in you and at the same time stand up and be counted with the best of them when it comes to day-in-day-out work on the river. I tell you this with the assurance of long experience, because the 20' White design is my personal canoe for my guided canoe trips on the Allagash and other Maine rivers.

Broad and deep, yet tapering to a narrow bow, the 20' White Guide design is a pleasure to handle with a load of 1,000 to 1,500 pounds or with just two paddlers out for a day's fun on the river or lake. The bow and stern may be a trifle high and the cause for concern in a crosswind, but I have never found this canoe to be bad in this respect. For sure, I would not want to alter that beautiful sheerline that makes the White so recognizable. Just how important is beauty in a working canoe? Of course, it has to be second to utility, but with the 20' White model there is no need to sacrifice one for the other. I highly recommend it.

The 18' White Guide model is actually an 18½' canoe. Why this odd length was used (canoes are more often designed with an overall length in even feet) is open to question; maybe it reinforces the claim that E. M. White copied the old Indian designs, which would have been made with measurements known mainly to them. I wish I had the words or the artistic ability to express the beauty I see in the lines of this canoe. Since I am a lifelong hunter and lover of wildlife, I can best express it in terms of deer: I think of the 20-footer as a large, beautiful, and powerful buck; the 18-footer would be his smaller, more graceful, but just as beautiful doe.

I want to emphasize that these are two completely different canoes, and not a case where one design has been altered to produce another (except possibly by Mr. White almost a century ago). For the White Guide, you will do best to use the pattern for the canoe you need. (Exception: In one of my evening adult classes, one of the builders nailed his stations for an 18-footer to the wrong side of the strongback [the 20" spacing instead of 18"]. None of us noticed it until the canoe was about half stripped. It looked pretty good, so the fellow decided to go on with it. The result was a beautifully proportioned, slender 20-footer that he was delighted with. We have purposely used the technique since that time. But, if you want a big canoe for big water and heavy work, then go for the 20' pattern.)

When my students come to class with definite ideas as to the canoe they want to build, we come as close to it as possible. However, more often than not they come asking me for my recommendation. After a little questioning to correctly determine their needs, I find that nine times out of ten I end up advising them to build a White design, usually the 18-footer. None to my knowledge have ever regretted this choice. If you want the closest thing to an all-around canoe that is beautiful to look at as well as functional, then look no farther than one of these White designs.

16

The River Canoes

Specifications:	White Water	River Runner
Length	16′ 0″	19′ 0″
Width	36″	39½″
Depth	12¾″	14″
Height of stems	24″	25″
Approximate weight	65 lbs	90 lbs

Whenever you look at the profile of a canoe and a banana comes to mind, you are looking at a canoe designed to be used primarily in moving water. The Eastern Cree Indians in Canada built a canoe that was literally banana-shaped, having rocker that extended the entire length of the canoe. The modern rockered canoe has the up-turn for the last three or four feet at each end, the center portion of the canoe remaining fairly flat.

If you need rocker — that is, if you do almost all of your canoeing in moving water — the two models described here are great for river running. I have used both of them for years and can attest to their performance in whitewater. However, the rocker that allows you to twist and turn so easily on the river becomes a barge-shaped bow on the lake that you must push through the water with each paddle stroke. I don't want to make it sound too bad, though, because in reality, the difference is not actually noticeable unless you are paddling across the lake beside another canoe that is better suited to that environment. So, my recommendation would be that if you will be in moving water *most* of the time, go for the river canoe. If you will spend at least half of your paddling time on flat water, then a more general-purpose canoe like the White designs will suit you.

The 16′ White Water was designed primarily for just good fun. We like to spend weekends in the early spring canoeing favorite whitewater rivers and streams in our area. This canoe is ideal for that purpose. It will handle two paddlers, without a significant amount of gear, on some pretty rough stretches of rapids. The White Water's usefulness is not limited to play, however. If your need is a solo canoe for whitewater tripping, I can think of none better suited to that purpose. It will take you and your gear over miles of whitewater river with minimum effort and insignificant splashes over the gunwale.

The 19′ River Runner is the tripping canoe for river trips or even combination trips. The nicely rockered ends allow for easy turning even when the canoe is heavily laden with gear and people, and the broad bow has a wonderful lift to it when the canoe pitches down — even when it dives into one of those dreaded foam-filled holes. Most canoes emerge from such places with at least a couple of gallons of river shifting around on the bottom, but the River Runner usually comes through high and dry.

These two canoes, like the two White designs, are completely separate designs and not merely an expansion or contraction of the same canoe. If you want one or the other, you will find it much easier to use the correct plan. Altering one to become the other requires extensive changes. However, if your need is for a slightly larger or smaller version of either model, then pick the plan closest to your needs, and go to it. It'll turn out fine.

The 19′ River Runner is a workhorse for lengthy river trips.

The square-sterned 19½' Grand Laker is a big canoe designed for power on big water.

The Grand Laker

Specifications:	
Length	19′6″
Width	45″
Depth	18″ (center)
Height of stems	26″
Approximate weight	135 lbs

It did not take long, after the first powered canoe appeared in the Grand Lake Stream area of Maine, for folks to become aware of its advantages — especially, the working guides in this popular fishing area. The first was a square-stern built by the Old Town Canoe Company in 1922, but before long, square-sterned canoes were being produced locally, and the process of evolution that would eventually produce a unique canoe was under way. This model combined the needed features of the traditional canoe with those of the big, motor-powered lake boat. The result was a big canoe — certainly not of a size and shape to lend itself to paddle power, but that was able to handle a motor of up to 10 horsepower and be steady and reliable on a big lake.

At first, many old-time guides would not have anything to do with the newfangled square-sterns. However, to compete with the extended range of the powered canoes, guides using the traditional double-enders had to rely on the steamboat *Woodchuck* to haul their canoes up the lake in the morning and back in the evening. It was not too long

before all of the guides in the area switched over. Of course, the fact that guides with powered canoes received $2.00 a day more than those with paddle-powered craft could have had something to do with the rapid acceptance of the canoe that was to become known as the Grand Laker.

Today, several molds exist for Grand Lakers, and several builders make them in Maine and perhaps elsewhere. I have to confess that this canoe is the only one in this book of which I have no firsthand knowledge. It isn't that I have anything against motor-powered canoes; it is just that my work and pleasure do not require a canoe of this type. When I need an outboard, a motor bracket on my double-ender does very well; but friends and former students who do use this design tell me it does a great job, and so on the strength of their endorsement I offer the pattern to you.

The Wabnaki

Specifications:	
Length	16′
Width	36″
Depth	12½″
Height of stems	18″
Approximate weight	65 lbs

The Wabnaki is named for our Maine and New Brunswick Indians — not because I claim any sort of authenticity for the shape, but because I have a strong interest in these people, and the canoe

The 16' Wabnaki is a good solo canoe. The ends on this canoe were modified to more closely resemble those of the Indian canoes. It also diminishes wind-catching surface area. The modification was made after the stations were removed.

reminds me of some of their medium-sized canoes I have seen pictured. Also, the intended use for the canoe had a bearing on the name I chose. I wanted what is commonly called a "solo" canoe — big enough for one person to use for an extended trip, yet small enough that handling it would not be a major undertaking each day. Since it would be handled on the water by one person, the bow and stern had to be low so as not to catch wind and send it spinning. It was a canoe for the independent loner — the person who enjoyed going it alone. This — the sort of person the canoe was intended for, as much as the shape — was responsible for the name.

I always hesitate to recommend a canoe shorter than 18' for an extended canoe trip. I am a "big-canoe man," so to speak. However, the experienced person who wants to go it alone will not need the additional length. The word "experience" is the key here. The experienced tripper knows how to pick his route on a windy day to minimize the effects of the wind and thus reach the destination for the day. By the same token, the experienced tripper knows when to stay ashore and when not to go out at all. The experienced tripper knows how to load the canoe to best trim it for the current conditions. I could go on with this, but you see my point. Know your canoe *and* your ability.

I am fond of this little canoe; otherwise, I wouldn't have named it for a people I admire. I think the bow and stern variations shown in the photo on this page give it character and make its name even more fitting. The design has possibilities for variations that you may be looking for. One might be to make it a little deeper if it is to be used for trips. The very popular Old Town Tripper is 15" deep and is 17' 2" long. I would say that the depth of the Wabnaki could easily be brought up to 14" without causing it to look out of proportion, but I have not experimented with this.

The Laker

Specifications:	
Length	16'
Width	36"
Depth	13"
Height of stems	22½"
Approximate weight	65 lbs

I started building strip canoes in the very early 1970s. At that time, I was casting about, looking for a canoe-building method that would lend itself to use by relatively unskilled high-school students with some guidance from me. A friend gave me a copy of *Popular Science* that contained an article on building a redwood canoe. That redwood canoe was what I have named "the Laker."

I see the Laker as a canoe for casual canoeing — maybe at a summer cottage, for occasional use by family members and for youngsters to gain experience by paddling around at their leisure. The flat cross-section makes the hull stable, and the flat

19

The Laker is a good general-purpose canoe. (The 13' version is shown here.) If I were to attach a keel to any canoe, this would be the one.

bottom from stem to stem almost suggests that it should have a keel. Of course, I make no bones about the fact that I feel a keel is an abomination on a canoe; but if any canoe *should* have a keel, it would be the Laker.

The forms for this canoe will build two different models, with absolutely no modification. From the nine stations for the 16' model, simply leave out the center station and one of its neighbors, and you have yourself a 13-footer. (Omit Stations 4 and 5, or 5 and 6.) All spacing and other measurements remain the same. In theory, you can do this with any set of stations for any model of canoe; but in reality, it is usually necessary to make minor changes to the stations so that the new length will come up smooth, with no waves or humps in the hull.

I have to say that the lines of the Laker do not really turn me on, but it is a very practical canoe that will serve well for its intended purpose. One of my adult students used this pattern as the basis for a canoe he wanted to design himself, and I was really impressed with his finished canoe. So, if you are inclined in that direction, look at each canoe design in this book in parts rather than as the whole canoe. In that way, you can alter the patterns by using the desired features of several to come up with your own dream canoe — that ever-elusive "ideal canoe." The "ideal" may continue to elude you, but you will have some fun, and with eight different models to choose from, you have quite a few possibilities to try before you run out of combinations.

The Puddle Duck

Specifications:	
Length	14'
Width	34½"
Depth	12"
Height of stems	20"
Approximate weight	45 lbs

Have you ever wanted a canoe for your own private use? I don't mean the family canoe or one to use for tripping where others will be with you, but one just for you — a canoe you can leave hidden at a favorite small stream or pond that will be there for you to use without any prior thought, preparation, or planning. Or maybe you are a trapper or hunter or fisherman who needs to get out on small bodies of water, but without the bother of handling a large canoe onto and off a vehicle by yourself.

The Puddle Duck is just the canoe for the situations described above. As such it might be called a "special-purpose" canoe, but I think it is too versatile to bear that label. It is small and light enough for an average person to handle alone both in and out of the water. It has the capacity to carry two people, if necessary, though it is better suited to one handler and his tools or gear for the day's work or play.

My own Puddle Duck has been in service since before the original *Building a Strip Canoe* was published. It is the one pictured in that book and in

The 14' Puddle Duck is the personal canoe, perfect for poking around those small ponds, streams, and marshes.

this one. I still use it on the little stream that borders our property. Part of every year it lies hidden in the alders near the stream where it is ready to use on a warm summer evening when I decide the evening's walk should be topped off with a short paddle on the quiet section of the stream. When deer season rolls around, my Puddle Duck changes from toy to tool, so to speak, when it is used for crossing or even hunting that same stream, or hopefully, to transport some locally grown venison to a convenient pick-up point. Only at the end of November when the deer season ends and ice locks the stream in its grip for the next several months does the little canoe come home to rest on the rack with the larger tripping canoes.

Of course, leaving a canoe hidden in the woods is not without risk. The little Puddle Duck in the picture was stolen from its hiding place and was gone for 14 months until a trapper friend of mine ran across it while checking his trap line. It was on the same stream, but miles from home. Since the canoe was unique, and he recognized it instantly, he did not hesitate to hoist it up and carry it to his pickup. Later that day, I saw the little canoe coming up my driveway. I still remember the feeling — like a member of the family coming home. The little canoe went back to stream-side, but I'm a little more careful how I hide it.

The strongback, ready for the stations to be nailed on.

The Preliminaries

Preparing to start a large project almost always involves a considerable amount of work that seems unproductive in itself, but is nevertheless necessary. In the case of building a strip canoe, not only are the preliminaries necessary, but it is essential that they be done well if the finished product is to be one that you can be proud of. The strongback and the stations are nothing more than tools to be used in the construction of your canoe. As such, they will have no function once the canoe is finished any more than will your hammer and saw. However, like your other tools, their quality has much to do with the quality of your work. It is very difficult to do quality work with shoddy tools. The strips, of course, are a part of the finished canoe, but are mentioned here because sawing them out is a dusty job that is nice to have behind you once the fun stuff — the stripping — begins.

The Strongback

The first thing you will need is the strongback, the spine that holds the stations and stem forms in place. Around this temporary frame you will build the body of your canoe. Built of 2×6s and 2×4s with some $1''$ boards for bracing, the strongback should be long enough for the biggest canoe that you are likely to want. (You can always build a short canoe on a long strongback, but not the other way around. Take a look at Figure 2, and you will see that the strongback can be at most $2'$ shorter than the canoe you will build.)

Don't bother trying to find $20' 2 \times 6$s if you want to build a 20-footer. Just spike together two $12'$ pieces with a $3'$ overlap, to end up with $18'$. You will find this plenty strong, and avoid the expense of unusually long lumber.

Cut enough $18''$ lengths of 2×4 for the number of stations you plan to have. The usual spacing is $18''$ or $20''$, but this can be adjusted, within reason, toward any final length. Be sure to space the 2×4s from the same side each time and to nail the stations to that side.

Look at Figure 2; it shows the correct layout and spacing for a $16'$ canoe. With stations $18''$ apart, note that the end of the stem forms will be $24''$ from Stations 1 and 9. Fourteen-foot 2×6s will be long enough to build a $16'$ canoe. Put in two or three diagonal braces, as shown in Figure 2, to help make the strongback more rigid; nail these braces to cleats inside the 2×6s.

This same strongback and set of stations would build a $13'$ or $14'$ canoe, at least in theory. To build a 13-footer, simply eliminate Stations 5 and 6; then make Station 4 the center station. The stem form and everything else would have the same spacing. The reason I said "in theory" is that in most cases this kind of shortening (or lengthening) results in the need for some minor adjustments in the stations to ensure a smooth hull without waves or bumps. Once they have been altered for the new length, these stations are unfit for their original purpose. Figure 3 shows the $13'$ setup. The station numbers in parentheses show how they were originally numbered in the $16'$ setup. (Usually we re-number from 1 to 7 rather than using the numbers from the longer strongback, to avoid confusion.)

A 14-footer will require a different spacing of the seven stations. This works out to be a $20''$ space, so turn the strongback over and use the other side with a new set of $18'' 2 \times 4$ pieces. This way, you will not have to disturb the $18''$ spacing which you may want to use in the future. Besides, it is difficult to avoid splitting and thus ruining the

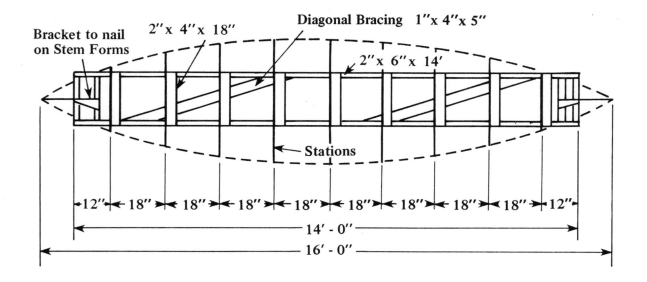

Bracket to nail on Stem Forms

2" x 4" x 18"

Diagonal Bracing 1" x 4" x 5"

2" x 6" x 14'

Stations

←12"→←18"→←18"→←18"→←18"→←18"→←18"→←18"→←18"→←12"→

14' - 0"

16' - 0"

SCALE: 3/8 " = 1' - 0"

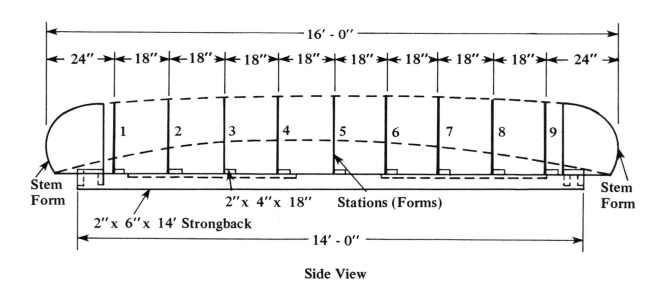

16' - 0"

←24"→←18"→←18"→←18"→←18"→←18"→←18"→←18"→←18"→←24"→

1 2 3 4 5 6 7 8 9

Stem Form

Stem Form

2" x 4" x 18"   Stations (Forms)

2" x 6" x 14' Strongback

14' - 0"

Side View

FIGURE 2 · Strongback with Locations of Stations and Stem Forms

24

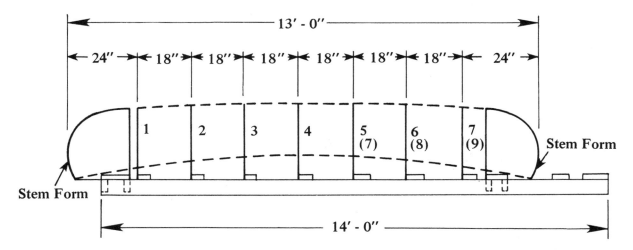

FIGURE 3 · Setup for a 13' Canoe, with Strongback and Stations for a 16-Footer

2×4s when removing them. (By the way, this is why we nailed those braces to cleats on the inside of the strongback instead of to the bottom.) You will probably have to remove one of the 18" 2×4 pieces for the shorter canoe, to make room for the stem form.

Another way the length can be altered is to set the stem forms in or out. A 6" change in each will result in a 1' difference in the overall length of the finished canoe. Bear in mind, though, that this method can considerably alter the shape of the canoe in the bow and stern, depending on the amount of change. Minor length changes by either method will not show any noticeable change in the canoe's final shape.

For longer canoes you will need a longer strongback, but the layout is the same. With two more stations (total of 11) at the 18" spacing, for example, you will end up with a 19' canoe. Eleven stations at the 20" spacing will build a 20' canoe if you move the stem forms in so that they measure 20" from Stations 1 and 11. By making minor adjustments in station spacing and by moving the stem forms in or out a little, you can come up with virtually any length. I have never found it necessary to use other than the 18" or 20" station spacing, however. It is usually easier to figure in inches than in feet. A 20' canoe is 240". With 10 spaces between stations at 20" each, for a total of 200", 40" are left to divide between the two stem forms.

The strongback will last indefinitely if you take care of it. Keep it out of the weather and be sure to store it lying flat so as not to put a twist in it. Once

the strongback has warped, twisted, or whatever, it is nearly impossible to get it back into shape. All you can do is salvage what lumber you can and start over.

> **Summary of materials and tools needed to build a strongback for a 16' canoe:**
>
> **Materials**
>
> | | |
> |---|---|
> | 2 pieces 2"×6"×14' | 16d common nails |
> | 2 pieces 2"×4"×10' | 8d common nails |
> | 1 piece 1"×4"×10' | |
>
> **Tools**
>
> | | |
> |---|---|
> | Rule | Hammer |
> | Pencil | Framing square |
> | Handsaw or power handsaw | |

The Stations

The stations or forms give your canoe its shape. A sloppy job of making them will cause all manner of problems later on, so it is important that you take care to trace your pattern accurately. Something that helps keep things straight and true is a framing square. Use it to draw the centerline of each station, instead of just depending on the edge of the paper pattern. This way, you are sure each centerline is square with the bottom edge of the station. Keep these centerlines clearly visible on the

25

finished stations; they are handy later on.

Except for the center one, each station has a twin on the other end of the canoe, and each pattern represents one half of a station. There are exceptions; sometimes canoes are built with the stern a little fuller than the bow. This means that the stern would look something like the freighter-shaped canoe in Figure 1, while the bow would be more like the streamlined one. This has some advantage when operating in shallow water; and when a motor is mounted at the stern, the fullness gives a little extra flotation to support the additional weight. None of the patterns in this book are of this type, however. The Grand Laker is an exception: each of its stations is unique.

The stations are made of ½″ plywood. Buy CDX plywood (sheathing); this will be the least expensive. I have tried the material sold under the trade name of Aspenite, which is a sheathing made up of wood flakes and small chips bonded together. It is less expensive than CDX plywood, but was not satisfactory, the staples could not hold in it. You will need two sheets for either a 9- or 11-station canoe. Lay your patterns out carefully and plan so as to have the least amount of waste, then cut the stations out with a saber (bayonet) saw or a bandsaw. Once you have the stations done, you have to make the stem forms. These are usually made of ¾″ plywood — the extra thickness is needed for strength and substance when the strips are attached to the stem form.

There is no reason why the stem forms couldn't be 1″ thick instead of ¾″ thick; by piecing scraps of leftover ½″ plywood, you could save the expense of a sheet of ¾″ plywood. Cut out twice as many forms as needed from your ½″ plywood, and glue and nail these together. You will have plenty of plywood to do this if you are building a 9-station canoe. If you are building an 11-station canoe, you might have to piece together some scraps for double the area, but as long as they are glued and nailed together the stem form will be sturdy enough.

Once you have your stem forms cut out, the curved edge has to be brought to a point. (Figure 4 shows this in cross section; you can also see it in the photo on page 35. You will have to estimate the angle for this, but it is not too critical — it would take a gross error to affect the shape of the canoe. A coarse rasp will do a good job of removing the wood to get a pointed cross section.

For later convenience, you should number your stations, and mark them as to the size and type of canoe they are designed to build. If you build

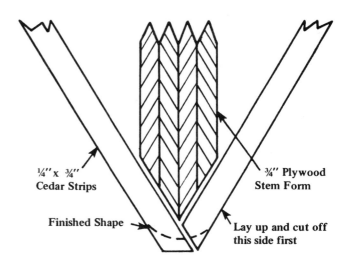

**FIGURE 4 · Fitting Strips to the Stem Form
See photo on page 35.**

¼″ x ¾″ Cedar Strips

¾″ Plywood Stem Form

Finished Shape

Lay up and cut off this side first

canoes of other shapes and sizes later on, you will be glad you did. Also, it never hurts to have your name on them in case you loan them out.

The stations can be used for a long time. I have never kept track of how many canoes a set will build, but I'm sure it is a considerable number. They do get kind of ragged on the edge after a couple of trillion staples and nails have been in and out of them, especially on the lower edge where the first strip goes and on the top of the first and second stations of each end where nails are usually needed to hold the strips in place. I have extended the usefulness of some of my forms by gluing and nailing a block of wood on the lower edge so that I could drive the nail and staple into the block instead of the plywood. Also, when the plywood edge gets frayed, I just tack on a scrap piece of plywood and re-cut it, following the old one as a pattern. Unless you build a lot of canoes on your stations, though, probably none of this maintenance will be necessary.

Summary of materials and tools needed to build the stations:

Materials

2 sheets of ½″ CDX plywood

A 2′ × 4′ piece of ¾″ plywood (optional, see text)

Tools

Framing square	Paper patterns
Pencil	Coarse wood rasp
Sabersaw or bandsaw	

The Strips

The choice of wood from which to make the strips depends upon where you live. Most often, a wood native to your area will be less expensive than an imported species. However, even though I live about as far from California as one can get, I have built canoes of redwood. You have a wide choice.

I have used four different woods: redwood, white pine, white cedar, and basswood. Of these four I prefer the cedar, head and shoulders above the others. It is lightweight — an important factor in the finished canoe. It is limber; this means it bends easily during construction and also gives a degree of flexibility to the finished canoe. And, white cedar has a pleasing variety of colors when finished naturally. Redwood, besides being expensive, is rather brittle and breaks easily during construction. I often found it necessary to soak the redwood strips for a few minutes to ensure against breakage. Pine bends well, but is heavier than the cedar and offers no advantage that I can see, except perhaps easy availability. Basswood is a much-overlooked wood these days. Years ago, woodworkers relied upon it for a variety of uses because it is easy to work with, light in weight, and clear boards were easily available. The only fault I can find with basswood for strip-canoe building is that it is a little heavier than cedar, and the grain and coloration are not as attractive or as interesting as those of the cedar.

The Northern White Cedar (*Thuja occidentalis*) is not generally available in long lengths because the tree tapers sharply. This means it is not economically feasible to saw long boards. Ten-footers are usually about the longest, but this is no disadvantage. Simply make a butt joint wherever it may fall; you needn't make the joints on the stations. (They won't be there when the canoe is done, anyway, remember?) Just be sure that you break your joints. This means, don't let them fall along the same vertical line, or there will appear to be a seam in the finished canoe. Use random lengths to prevent this, even going so far as to cut a long strip to achieve the breaks.

In Appendix I, I have listed some sources of supplies and materials, including wood, but I strongly urge you to thoroughly exhaust all possible local sources before ordering from away.

Whatever wood you use, you will need about 48 board feet for a 16′ canoe and about 60 board feet for a 20-footer. These quantities are meant only as a guide, but they should be more than enough — unless you buy really low-quality stock and have a lot of waste. It takes somewhere in the neighborhood of 75 to 80 strips to plank the canoe. Remember that this means a strip the full length of the

Sawing the ¼″ cedar strips.

hull, so for a 20-footer it would take almost two and a half 10′ pieces to go the length of it. Do your math, and you'll see that it will take up to 200 10′ strips to plank a 20-footer.

Unless you have a surface planer, you should buy the boards finished to ¾″ or 7/8″ thickness. The thickness of your boards will determine the final width of your strips. For most of my canoes I use 7/8″ strips, but for some (the two river canoes, for example), the ¾″ thickness works better. For these canoes, the combination of the rocker and the sheerline gives the strips so much edge-bend that the ¾″ width is recommended. If you buy your lumber rough, be sure it is thick enough so that it can be planed to the desired thickness. If you don't have a local woodworking shop that will plane it for you, try your high-school or vocation-school shop. Most instructors might be happy to plane out small quantities at their convenience.

Once you have your finished lumber, all that is necessary is to set the rip fence of the table saw for ¼″ thickness and start stripping. What you end up with is a lot of little boards (strips) ¼″ × ¾″ (or 7/8″) × 10″, or whatever length. If you have knots in the cedar, they may cause the strips to break, but you want random lengths anyway, to break your joints. All you need to do is square up the ends when you use them. And, be careful when ripping strips to keep the ¼″ thickness uniform throughout the length of the piece. Thin spots are bad news!

Generally, it is best to have two people to do the stripping, but you can handle it alone if you set up a rest to receive the board as it comes off the saw. Without this rest, you will have to use a lot of down-pressure as you approach the end of the board. This strain on you could cause a slip and an accident. Use a push-stick when you get near the end of the board, especially when the board is nearly used up. A good rule to remember when using the table saw is to never have the saw blade more than ¼″ above the surface being cut; this way, if you *should* have an accident, you would only be cut ¼″ deep. Bad enough, but better than losing a whole finger.

Once you have all of your strips made, put them where they will not get walked on or otherwise abused, as they are rather fragile. Bring them out a few at a time as you use them.

Summary of materials and tools needed to make the strips:

Materials

48 to 60 board feet of ¾″ or 7/8″ boards (wood of your choice)

Tools

Rule	Push-stick
Table saw with sharp blade	Safety goggles

Building the Hull

Now that you have those boring (but important) preliminaries over with, it is time to start putting things together and watch your canoe take shape. To me, this is the most exciting part of building a canoe — watching it grow into a beautiful, sleek, yet extremely functional form. It is the same whether it is a model that I have built many times before, or a new design that I am trying for the first time. After watching over 200 of them take shape, I still thrill to see it.

Stripping

Start by setting the strongback on a couple of sawhorses to raise it to a convenient height. Next, take Stations 1 and 9 and mount them in their proper places at each end of the strongback. Be sure they are centered on the 2 × 4 crosspieces, and that the centerline is vertical. Now drive a small nail in the top center of Stations 1 and 9, and stretch a line tautly between them. You can get this line tighter if you anchor it to the end of the strongback after passing it around the center nail on the stations. Stations 2 through 8 are centered on this line — not on the strongback. The use of the line ensures that the canoe will be straight, even though the strongback may have warped out of line a little.

It is best to use double-headed or staging nails to mount the stations so that they can be easily removed when the time comes. If you cannot obtain these nails, let the heads of regular nails protrude enough so that you can get ahold of them with the claw of a hammer.

If you are building a Grand Laker, everything will be set up about the same except that the square stern is to be a permanent part of the finished hull. Make it from 1½ " oak or ash. It is okay to glue up

pieces with waterproof glue to obtain the required width. Place the stern at 10° from vertical, with the top (as it sits on the strongback, actually the bottom of the canoe) leaning toward the bow. The stern is held in place at the proper height by a piece of plywood, as indicated in the plans. Once the stern is positioned and held at the proper angle, you should relieve the edge so that it will receive the strips flush without leaving a gap on the inside. (See Figure 5.)

Now, with all of the stations in place, take the stem forms and mount them in the center of the strongback and at the proper distance from Stations 1 and 9. If you are building one of the White models, the Wabnaki, or the Grand Laker, the stem forms are made to the correct length, so they may be butted directly against the first and last station and nailed to them. For the other models, nail on extenders as shown in Figure 6, and do the same. This makes a much more solid setup and is easier to put together. Otherwise, you could extend the end forms to the required length when you are making them from the patterns. Also shown in Figure 6 is a toe-nail put into the strongback instead of into a bracket. This makes it easier to get everything apart when the time comes, and yet it holds the stems solidly.

Use masking tape to cover the edges of the plywood stations and the stem forms. This prevents the glue from sticking to the forms, so that you can easily remove the hull. Be sure to apply a wide band of tape to each side of the stem form where the strips will touch it. Next, take a scrap piece (or pieces) of board or strapping, and lay it down the center of the stations (keel line). Put a nail through it into each station, making sure that the station is standing upright. When you have all

The stations are aligned to a taut line, not to the strongback.

Lining up the stations on the strongback.

Now that the preliminaries are complete, you are ready to start stripping.

of the stations held firmly in place by this temporary keel, stand back and sight along the stem forms to make sure they are vertical and parallel with the keel line. Hold each one in place as you put a nail through the temporary keel and into the stem form.

Eyeball the whole thing! All should look straight and symmetrical. Usually any error that has been made can be spotted by a critical eye at this point. If everything looks well aligned, you are ready to start putting on the strips.

The first strip establishes the sheer of the canoe. Choose good, clear strips for this first one. Generally it is necessary to nail this strip in places with small (2d) nails, because the staples will not hold until there is a previous strip to help support

the current one. When the first strip is on, walk around it, squat down and peer at it, stand and sight along it until you are satisfied that it looks right. The sheerline and depth of the canoe are established by the stations, but it is possible to make minor modifications at this time if you wish. Most often you just have to ensure a clean, symmetrical line.

If you are building a shorter canoe, using stations from a long one, you should check on the depth at the center of the hull. Many canoe hulls get progressively deeper as you move from the center toward the ends. This means that Station 4 in Figure 2, which becomes the center station in the 13′ setup in Figure 3, might be deeper than you wish the center of the small canoe to be. If this is the case, simply mark the desired depth on the stations and start your first strip on these marks instead of at the lower edge of the stations. You can change the sheerline, or make the whole canoe a little shallower.

Next, lay a bead of white glue along the edge of the first strip and press the next strip into it. Staple the strip in place with 9/16″ staples. You will probably find that it is necessary to put one or two staples between the stations, as well as one into the stations, to keep the strips aligned with each other. Some folks like to use two staplers, one loaded with 9/16″ staples, and the other loaded with 1/4″ staples. They use the shorter ones between the stations where length isn't needed to reach through to a station. I have tried this, and found it cumber-

FIGURE 5 · Setting Up and Trimming the Stern of the Grand Laker

Trial strip

To be removed.

Lay each trial strip over at least the first two stations.

Next, measure this distance and transfer to the base of the stern here.

Now, a series of these marks can be made and connected, giving a line that will show the correct angle for the stern all along its curved surface.

10°

Stern screwed to plywood.

Strongback

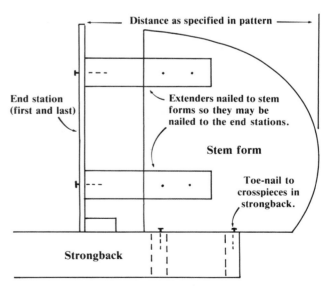

FIGURE 6 · Mounting Stem Forms
For Puddle Duck, Laker, White Water, and River Runner. Other models may be nailed directly, without extenders.

Distance as specified in pattern

End station (first and last)

Extenders nailed to stem forms so they may be nailed to the end stations.

Stem form

Toe-nail to crosspieces in strongback.

Strongback

The first strip is nailed in place along the sheerline.

Soon you will be able to almost run as you apply the bead of glue to the edge of the strip.

Keep the strips lined up with as many staples as necessary — no more!

some. Then, too, I sometimes use the technique of bending over the ends of a staple (like a paper staple) to increase its holding power in difficult-to-hold places.

Use a small nail at the stations if the staples will not hold adequately. Put on about six strips in this manner, on one side; then stop and trim the ends as shown in Figure 4 and in the photos on page 35. Symmetrically, lay up six strips on the other side. As you continue to strip the hull, you'll need to trim the ends every time you switch sides.

Sometimes the first few strips have a nasty habit of twisting near the ends, between the last couple of stations. This happens because there is quite a bend on them edgewise, with nothing firm to support them. If this occurs, use a couple of pieces of wood and a C-clamp until the glue hardens, and this will take care of it. (See photo on page 34.) I always like to lay up the same side first so that the angle cut as shown in Figure 4 will be on the same side all the way up the stem form. This is not too important, however.

If I were to make one general, all-encompassing statement about stripping, it would be this: do what you need to do to make the strips stay where you want them. If one staple does it, fine. If it takes a nail, use it. If a C-clamp is required, then by all means screw it on. Also, make sure to break your joints by using random lengths. You want to avoid the lining up of joints.

As you proceed up over the sharply curved bilge area of your canoe, it will become more and more obvious to you that you are putting flat, square strips on a curved surface. Gaps between strips will

On some models, the sharp edge-bend causes some problems at first. Do whatever is necessary to keep the strips lined up.

plane **6A(b)**. You need only concern yourself with those strips that go over the curved surface of the hull. This is best done by the trial-and-error method, taking off a little wood and then checking for fit. It doesn't take too long, because the cedar is soft and shapes easily.

Probably the best method of preparing strips is to bead and flute them **(c)**. Unfortunately, unless you are going to make several canoes, the trouble and expense of setting up the equipment for this operation it isn't very practical. A router set up on a table, or a wood shaper, is required, and special cutters must be used. I made my first cutters by grinding and shaping some old router cutters until they did the job. I later found a commercial source of cutters and bought a set of them. (The supplier is included in Appendix I.) Beaded and fluted strips have the added advantage of not requiring as many staples to hold the strips in place, as one strip helps hold the next one, and when stripping is completed

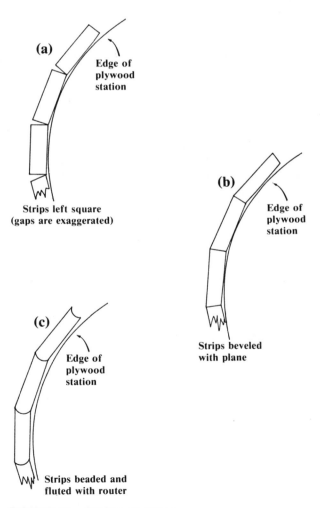

FIGURE 6A · Fitting of Strips

show up, as illustrated in Figure 6A **(a)**. The situation is not as serious as it might seem in the drawing, because the gaps usually fill with glue. As you shape and smooth the canoe, the size of the gaps diminishes; when the canoe is finished you will hardly know the gaps are there. Very likely, a slight crack of light will show through in some places when you look up through the finished canoe into strong light. These small light ''leaks'' do absolutely no harm, of course, but you may wish to use one of the other methods of fitting strips shown in Figure 6A. In any case, be sure, when stripping over the sharper curves of the stations, to make each strip lie as flat against the station as possible. The upper portion of the strip will tend to lift away, causing trouble when it is time to put on the next one.

One alternative is to bevel the strips with a block

Saw the strips like this so that the finished end will . . .

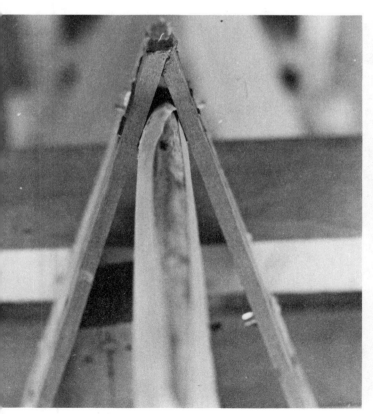

. . . look like this.

If it takes a nail to keep a balky strip in place, use it.

Here's the hull, over half-stripped.

The strips alternate, making a neat "seam" down the keel line.

Take care in fitting the strips as you work over the stem form.

On some models, especially the Whites, narrow strips help to make the transition over the stem. I darkened the seams for this photo so the narrow strips would stand out.

the hull requires less scraping and smoothing than with other methods.

On some models, the Whites especially, but on others too, it is difficult to fit the strips together as they come up over the stem form. Within a few strips, you are making the transition from a primarily vertical lay to a horizontal one. I have found narrow "half strips" to be the best answer to this problem. Strip out eight or ten strips that are exactly one-half as wide as normal, and use these to make the transition over each end of the canoe. (See above photo.) Then simply square up the ends of two adjoining half-strips so that a full strip will butt them. Continue the strip down the bottom of the hull, joining the other set of half-strips at the opposite end.

Once the transition from vertical to horizontal is complete, you will start alternating the strips from one side to the other, fitting the ends as you go along. This gives a nice-looking seam down the keel line of the canoe, as you can see in the photos on page 36. Continue laying strips and fitting the ends until the hull is completely closed in.

As you examine the canoe at this point, you will probably find some waves and minor irregularities.

However, unless these are very serious, they have a way of taking care of themselves with the sanding and subsequent operations. Once in a while there occurs a serious problem that requires modification of the offending station. This can almost always be accomplished before the stripping progresses too far. Usually this problem has been caused by a miscalculation or a slip made while tracing the stations from the pattern. Once a set of stations has been proven to produce a smooth hull, they can be used over and over; and when the edges are frayed beyond hope, they can be traced onto a new piece of plywood. Or sometimes, the frayed edge can be repaired by scarfing on a scrap piece of plywood and reshaping the edge.

When the strips are all laid up and the glue is dry, it is staple-pulling time! Use a screwdriver and pliers or whatever tool you can devise to do this tedious job. Also, remove any nails that you had to use to hold the strips in place. Once all of the hardware has been removed and nothing but glue is holding the thing together, you are ready for the smoothing operation.

Smoothing Up

Finally, you can see the shape of your canoe! It is like a gem in the rough, but still, the beauty is there. By now you are obsessed with the canoe-building, and your spouse is resigned to the fact that nothing else will get done around the homestead until the blasted thing is finished. When this happens, you might get that extra pair of hands you've been needing. Smoothing and sanding can be very boring. On the other hand, I think it is exciting — this is where you bring the canoe from its rough state to a beautiful, smooth shape.

Before you start sanding, you have to get rid of the excess glue and smooth up the irregularities in the strips so that you have a continuous, even surface. To do this I have tried several tools. I have used a disc sander with a very coarse sandpaper, but the glue clogs the paper too fast for it to be practical. An ordinary carpenter's plane works all right by itself, but the glue is hard on the plane, and it requires constant adjustment and resharpening. I found the best tools for the job to be the least expensive. A good-quality paint scraper works just fine. A couple of licks with a file every few minutes keeps it sharp, and it will take off that extra glue as well as dress down the soft cedar strips so that sanding will be minimized. The scrapers I use are Red Devil® numbers 3050 and 3055, which should serve you well. If a handle breaks, a replacement

The scrapers will at the same time remove excess glue and level off the cedar strips in preparation for the sanding operation.

can be easily fashioned from hardwood and will last indefinitely; you only need to buy replacement blades.

Sometimes the scraper chatters due to the arrangement of the grain in the wood. For these places I like the flat Stanley Surform[1] plane. It is a little slower, but does a good job of smoothing up.

Don't overdo the smoothing up. Remember, you only have ¼" strips to start with. Just bring the strips down to where they are all level and present a smooth surface — no more! Don't be too concerned if you chip out or gouge a depression too deep to remove. You have to do some filling a little later anyway, and you can take care of it then. Also, the fiberglass screeds the resin and serves as a wonderful filler of depressions and hider of mistakes. Work carefully and methodically over the whole hull with the scraper, and then plane or Surform where needed, until you have removed all

[1]Stanley and Surform are both registered trademarks of Stanley Tool, a Division of Stanley Works.

of the excess glue and wood, and the canoe's surface has begun to take shape.

Before you start sanding, go to the stems and shape them up with your Surform. First, get down and look at the stem in profile. Its line is, no doubt, uneven. Take the Surform and work the high spots down until the line is smooth from the keel line to the end. Now give the stem a small curve like that shown in the finished shape (broken line) in Figure 4. This curve is important when it comes time to fiberglass, so maintain it throughout the sanding operation, or leave it squared off *until* the sanding operation.

For sanding, use a power sander of some sort. I use a good-quality orbital sander with 36-grit (very coarse) paper. This does a good job, and does it fast. A belt sander will work well too, but I prefer the orbital sander because it is easier to control and is not as likely to cause waves and undulations. If you like, change paper and sand a little smoother with a finer paper, but you needn't do too much — the scratches that are caused by the 36-grit paper will not show when the fiberglass is on. Suit yourself on this, but sanding down to a grit finer than 50 or 80 is a total waste of time.

When you have the hull very nearly sanded to your satisfaction, mix up some water-based wood putty and fill the knotholes, nail holes, chips, gaps, cracks, and any other openings. The brand of filler

A hand plane can also be used, but the glue is hard on the blade.

True up the ends with a rasp or Surform, then stand back and eyeball them to ensure a clean, smooth line.

Sanding with an orbital sander.

Filling with wood putty. Sand this when dry.

Give special attention to the ends, where so many strips meet.

I like best is Durham's because it most nearly matches the coloration of the cedar. If you have knotholes that are too big to hold putty, just reach inside and put a piece of masking tape over the hole, then fill it from the outside. When this has hardened, go over the hull again with the sander and give it a final lick. Now look at her! Ain't she beautiful?

(Note: There is an alternative to filling with wood putty. Read on into the chapter on fiberglassing to see how to do your filling at the same time as you apply the sealer coat of resin.)

Summary of materials and tools needed to build the hull:

Materials	Tools
Strongback	Tacker capable of driving 9/16″ staples (Arrow T-50)
1 set of plywood stations	
16d staging nails	Hammer
2d nails	Handsaw (fine-toothed)
Piece or pieces of strapping (canoe length)	Chalkline at least 16′ long
Masking tape	2 sawhorses
75 or 80 ¼″ or 7/8″ cedar strips	3 or 4 C-clamps
2 or 3 quarts of white (Elmer's) glue	Screwdriver (or whatever) to pull staples
9/16″ staples	Paint scraper
36-grit sandpaper (and other as desired)	Plane or Surform or both
Wood putty (Durham's)	Flat file (to sharpen scraper)
	Putty knife
	Power sander
	An extra pair of hands, if possible

Fiberglassing

My father always enjoyed telling about how Mother got him to remodel the whole kitchen just because one doorknob needed to be replaced. One new thing led to another, and another, and . . . . That's how I got started on this book. Excited and enthused about epoxy resins, I set out to simply amend and update the original *Building a Strip Canoe* to include the use of the new materials and tools. Then, one new thing led to another, and another, and . . . . So, the subject of this chapter is the doorknob that prompted this new, completely revised edition.

This chapter is divided into two parts. The first part deals with the use of epoxy materials for fiberglassing your strip canoe. The second part is especially for those individuals who choose to use polyester resins; it is much shorter, since only the differences in handling methods are discussed. Since I use WEST SYSTEM products for my own canoe building, the instructions and recommendations for epoxies are for those materials. I doubt there would be a significant difference in application techniques among the various brands of epoxy, but I haven't used the other brands, so I don't know whether this is true. If your chosen manufacturer recommends techniques that differ from those that I recommend, I suggest you follow their instructions.

When I first started using epoxy resin, I had already been building and fiberglassing strip canoes for 12 or 13 years. I was still humble about my knowledge of the chemistry of resins in general, but I felt my skill in handling and using them was at least equal to that of most other builders. So, when I decided to try out the epoxy resins, I felt confident of my ability to achieve a smooth and professional-looking job. I carefully read the man-ufacturer's instructions for mixing the material, but only made a quick scan of the instructions for application, feeling secure that my time-proven methods of handling polyester resin would stand me in good stead for the epoxy resin as well. What a shattering blow to my pride that first job turned out to be!

I had runs on top of runs. Hours were spent sanding to get the hull surface even close to being acceptably smooth. This done, another thin coat was applied only to produce more runs. Probably twice as much resin was used as was necessary, and in the end we had a serviceable canoe, but it was certainly no beauty, nothing to be proud of.

At first I blamed the resin. It was too thick, and I could not spread it thin enough with a brush. The stuff reminded me of very cold honey in consistency as compared with the thin, syrup-like polyester resin I was accustomed to using. I was tempted to give up the idea and go back to Old Dependable; so far, the only good thing I could see about the epoxy, as compared with the polyester, was that it didn't stink as badly. But I knew that the fiberglassed canoe with epoxy would be superior to one made with polyester, so I swallowed my pride and went back to the instructions. (When all else fails, read the instructions.) What follows is what I had to learn the hard way. If you follow these in-structions, I *know* your first wood-epoxy canoe will be a lot better than mine was.

Epoxy Resin

Before starting out with application of the materials, I want to say a little about them and the tools used to apply them. If you use WEST SYSTEM resins, you should buy the cloth from the same source. It is treated to be compatible with the resins, and you will have a better and longer-lasting canoe. Besides, the cost is competitive with that of cloth from other sources. I apply two layers of six-ounce cloth to the outside of the hull and one layer inside. That means you need cloth measuring three times the length of your canoe, providing you use the 60" cloth, which is wide enough to cover the entire width of all the canoes in this book except the Grand Laker. (For that model, you will need to add a little extra cloth at each side near the gunwale, but this can be done with trimmings, so there is no need to buy extra cloth.) Add at least one additional yard to the total cloth for waste and wraparound. So, if you are building a 16' canoe you will need 3 times 16', or 48'. Converted to yards, that is 16 yards. Add the one yard for waste and wraparound, and that comes to 17 yards of 60" glass fabric that you'll need for your 16-footer. Use the same method to figure cloth requirements for other lengths. Personally, I like to have an extra yard or two for other projects, possible future patching, and just plain insurance and peace of mind, but you suit yourself on this.

Because the fiberglassing materials are the most expensive items of the whole project, I have tried to be very careful in recommending quantities for you to use. I fully realize the inconvenience of running out as well as the expense of over-buying. However, please realize that I am basing the amounts on my own experience. The way you use the materials *could* have an effect on the quantities required. WEST SYSTEM resin is sold by the pound, so that is how I will talk about it. According to Gougeons' catalog, it takes about 24 pounds, or two group "B" units, of resin and hardener for a 17' canoe. Or, expressed another way, it takes one pound for every 15 square feet of surface area. I found this amount to be very close to what I used. My most commonly built canoe is the 18' White Guide model. I weighed the resin for several of these, and the total amount used came out to an average of about 22 pounds per canoe.

Bear in mind that I have had a considerable amount of experience in mixing and using the resin, and so I figure on having little waste. I consider the two pounds' margin very small if you are a first-time builder, and so I would recommend that you also buy an additional three pounds of resin and hardener, which is sold as an "A" unit, if you plan to build an 18' or longer canoe. Again,

my findings coincide with Gougeons' recommendations, which call for a 20-percent allowance for waste in buying resin. For a 16' or shorter canoe, the two "B" units should be sufficient. If you have leftover resin, there are other projects for which you can use this amazing stuff. The paddles in this book are one example. I have described how to make other canoe-related gear (waterproof kitchen packs, pack frame) in *The Canoe Guide's Handbook*.[1] You will obtain a considerable amount of scrap cloth from the trimming of your canoe to use for these projects.

The WEST SYSTEM catalog will give you the choice of either fast (#205) or slow (#206) hardener. I have always used the slow hardener, since I am never in a hurry for the material to cure, and I don't like to feel pressured to finish the job. Since they produce nearly identical results when cured, time is apparently the only distinction between the two hardeners.

Buy some colloidal silica or some Microfibers to make glue and filling material. The manufacturer recommends Microfibers to make an adhesive; I've had good luck with both. You just mix in the thickener until the desired consistency is reached. If you plan to fill with epoxy material, buy the Filleting Blend; it will more nearly match the light color of your white cedar canoe. If you wish to fill with this material rather than with the water putty as described in the previous chapter, follow the instructions below for sealing the canoe; then mix a little thickener with a little resin and use it as a filler on the wetted canoe. When the sealer and filler are cured, you are ready to sand lightly and then proceed with the fiberglassing. (I don't believe there is any real advantage to filling this way, except that it saves a step — you don't have to wait for the wood putty to dry before proceeding with the sealer coat.)

The list of WEST SYSTEM tools you will need was based on the assumption that there will be two people doing the job. Thus, two roller frames will be enough. They can be wiped off and used over and over. Just be sure to get them as clean as possible between uses so that the rollers will keep working. There is an extra roller pan in the list. Once in a while, one will break when you flex it to remove hardened resin, but usually the old stuff pops out clean and the pan can be used over and over. The 18 roller covers should be more than sufficient for the job, but (as with the resin they apply) it doesn't hurt to buy a few extras. The squeegees are the least expensive and yet the most useful tools for

[1]Gil Gilpatrick, *The Canoe Guide's Handbook* (Freeport, Maine: DeLorme Publishing Co., 1981).

wetting out fiberglass with WEST SYSTEM resin.

Leading the list of optional tools are the little Mini Pumps. I believe they save enough resin to pay for themselves, though I have no proof of this. WEST SYSTEM resin must be mixed with the hardener at a 5:1 ratio by weight, and the job of measuring is done by these little pumps. One squirt of each is the correct ratio. Use as many strokes of each as are needed for the job at hand. Without the pumps, you will have to either weigh the correct amounts and then mix them; or you can mix by volume, though there is a slight error here because of the differing density of the two liquids. If you choose to do the measuring by volume (this is what I did before I got a pump), the simplest way is to mark a stick in six equal increments. Hold the stick upright in a container having straight vertical sides (I use a one-pound coffee can); fill with resin to the fifth increment, then add hardener until reaching the sixth. The Mini Pumps are at their biggest advantage when a small quantity of resin is needed, as glue for a small touch-up. The 5:1 ratio is almost impossible to measure or weigh accurately in such small amounts; by hand, you'd end up mixing more than is needed, thus wasting a lot.

The poly mixing pots are reusable and convenient for mixing your resin, but you can use almost

Applying the sealer coat of resin. Put on enough so the wood can get all it can "drink" but not enough to cause runs.

any clean metal or plastic container. The gloves are recommended both to keep your hands out of the messy stuff and as a safety measure in case you might be sensitive to the material. Also, you may want to consider the protective cream that you will find listed in the WEST SYSTEM catalog. The other equipment you will need should be available locally. I trust you have read the chapter on safety before proceeding with this one; consider the safety precautions as very inexpensive insurance.

Sealer Coat (Epoxy:) Now we're ready to get going. If you have already filled the holes and cracks in your hull with wood putty, then smoothed and sanded, you are ready to apply the sealer coat of resin. This step is simplicity itself. Just mix the resin according to the recommended proportions and apply it to the smooth hull with a roller. But before proceeding, let's pause a minute and learn a little about the WEST SYSTEM resin.

When resin and hardener are mixed, an exothermic (heat-producing) polymerization reaction is begun. At room temperature, the ingredients will appear to stay in the same state as when they were first mixed for the duration of the pot life. This is usually 15 to 20 minutes for fast hardener, and about 30 to 40 minutes for slow hardener. Thereafter the mixture will thicken, beginning visibly to change from a liquid to a solid material. In five to nine hours, the epoxy mixture reaches a partial cure, being relatively free of tackiness. It can be sanded and shaped in 15 to 20 hours. At this point, it will appear that the reaction is complete, but actually there is a residual reaction which continues for the next five to seven days, causing the epoxy to become harder.

A number of factors can influence the cure schedule described above, and since I have no way of knowing conditions under which you will be working, I think it is important that you understand them.

The most important factor to understand is that in an exothermic reaction such as this, the speed of the reaction can be accelerated by adding heat to it and conversely, can be slowed down by withdrawing heat. For instance, if you are mixing epoxy on a hot day, you will find the reaction to be faster than anticipated; pot life is shorter and cure-up occurs much more rapidly. On the other hand, if you are working in a cold atmosphere, pot life will be slightly longer and cure-up time will be extended. The ambient temperature is helping to accelerate the reaction in the first instance and, in the second, is causing catalytic heat to be dissipated to the atmosphere more rapidly, thus slowing down the reaction.

The heat that is being created chemically in your resin can dissipate more rapidly if it is spread out than it can when left standing in a container. So, the sooner you get the resin spread onto the canoe, the more working time you will have. Remember, too, that your roller pan has many times the surface area that the mixing pot has, and so it will be a better place for unused resin to stay as you work. The more confined the container, the faster the catalytic heat will build up.

If you know that you will be working where the temperature will be well below the normal of around 22 °C, you may want to consider using the fast hardener. You could also keep the unmixed resin in a warm place and leave the mixed resin in the pot for three to five minutes to initiate a better catalytic heat build-up.

If excess heat is the problem, you will have to take steps to minimize the effect on your resin. As a rule of thumb, figure that for every 10 °C above room temperature, pot life and cure-up time are cut in half. In the case of above normal temperatures you will have to take steps to keep the resin cool, and do whatever is possible to slow down the cure time. The simplest solution is to wait for the optimum conditions, if that is possible.

I like to mix the resin in batches of not more than one to one-and-a-half pounds each. In the large poly mixing pot, this would be about three-quarters full, and a little less than that in a one-pound coffee can. The sealing does not take much time and so there is no need to use more than one roller, but later on, when you get to applying and wetting out the fiberglass fabric, try to have at least one other person to lend you a hand. Put the sealer on thickly enough so that the wood can take in all of the liquid it is capable of absorbing, but not so thickly as to cause runs. This is not hard when you use the roller, as it will spread the resin smoothly and allow you to maintain control. If you have opted to fill with thickened resin, you can take a small amount of leftover resin, thicken it, and proceed with that step as soon as the sealer is on.

At this point in time I have not determined that more than one sealer coat is necessary prior to application of the fiberglass fabric. However, if you should want the absolute maximum penetration of the wood before fiberglassing, the additional sealer may be warranted. The material has amazing penetrating ability. When you have finished the outside of your canoe and start smoothing the inside,

you will see a drop of hardened resin at each staple hole where it penetrated through the wood. The reason I have a small amount of doubt at this point is that after the fiberglass fabric is wetted out, there will be seen small bubbles rising to the surface which indicate more penetration of the resin into the wood. This bubbling is especially prevalent when the inside is being fiberglassed and the outside of the canoe has been sealed off. However, from what I have observed, this simply completes the job of wood penetration, and I have not seen the necessity for more sealer coats. The bubbles, if they persist after the resin has cured, can be quickly whisked away with sandpaper, and subsequent coats of resin will smooth out the surface.

In 15 to 20 hours, the sealer coat will be cured and you can go back to work again. All that remains for you to do before proceeding to the next step is to lightly sand the hull. Usually hand-sanding is sufficient, but you may use the power sander if you wish. In any case, do not sand through the resin into the bare wood, or you will partially undo what has been accomplished up to this point. Number 80-grit sandpaper is used, and all that is needed is to remove that "fuzzy" feeling and any dust particles that may have landed in the still-wet resin and stuck there. When the hull feels reasonably smooth as you run your hand over it, you are ready for the stem reinforcement.

Stem Reinforcement: Since strip canoes have no inside stempiece, as do other wood canoes, I recommend that additional reinforcement be applied here in the form of extra fiberglass fabric. Some builders of traditional (rib-and-plank) canoes have been critical of this method, saying that they would like to see a hardwood stempiece installed in the stems. I have considered this, and still feel that my method is best for this kind of canoe. I have used the strip canoes extensively and have had them wrecked beyond repair. Yet, in no case did the stem portion of the canoes, which we used and abused, show signs of failure.

You will need two strips of fiberglass fabric about 5″ wide and 3′ to 3½′ long. Cut two more strips about the same width and 1½′ to 2′ long. If the only cloth you have is what you bought in the 60″ width, just cut a strip from each *side* of the end of the fabric (making it 50″ wide instead of 60″ wide at that point). When the cloth is applied to the canoe, there is a lot more fabric than you will need at each end where the canoe narrows, so you are just borrowing what will be cut off later, anyway.

Fiberglass tape is available in 3″, 4″, and 6″ widths

which you can use for stem reinforcement if you wish, but there is no necessity for this expense. Your scraps will do just as well.

The longest strip should be placed and folded right over the stem, starting at the top (it is the bottom now, though) where it meets the strongback, and should extend well around to the bottom of the canoe, covering the portion of the canoe that will often take a lot of abrasion when the canoe is skidded ashore onto sand and gravel. The shorter strip also goes here for extra reinforcement, making two layers of fiberglass to be put on that critical area before the main layers of fabric are applied.

You will have to cut slits in the cloth to make it lie flat around the sharp curve of the stem, but this is normal, and the roughness this creates can be sanded away when the edges of the reinforcement are feathered in preparation for the main fiberglassing job.

Since this is such a small fiberglassing job, I usually wet the cloth out with a foam brush rather than use up a roller cover. However, this is an economy move, and the job will go faster with both. You will find that the fabric has a lot of bias "stretch," and by pushing, pulling, and teasing it around you can make it take almost any reasonable shape. Two sets of slits in your strips will be sufficient. The "stretch" of the cloth will accommodate the rest of the shaping.

When your reinforcing strips have cured, sand them with 50- or 80-grit sandpaper to remove any roughness and to feather out their edges. Be careful when feathering not to sand through your sealer coat where the strip meets the wood. This feathering and smoothing need not be carried to the extreme of smoothness; the fiberglass to come will act as a screed and cover up a lot of the irregularity. Just be sure there are no rough edges to catch the fabric or create bubbles under the next layer of fabric that you are soon to apply. Now you are ready for the main event!

Fiberglassing the Hull (Epoxy): Start by just draping the fiberglass fabric over the canoe and cutting the ends so that there are about 6″ of fabric extending beyond the stems. You will see already that the fabric tends to assume the shape of the hull. There will be some waves in the cloth near the gunwale area; take care of this by tugging gently at the fabric from up near the stems. Be sure that everything you do to make the fabric behave and assume the shape you desire is done with gentleness. The cloth will respond well to careful treatment, but if you are rough with it, it will crinkle,

The stem reinforcement is in place. Note the slits that allow the strip to come smoothly around.

wrinkle, and defy you every step of the way.

When you have one layer laid out smoothly, put the other right over it. That's right — you will wet out both of them at the same time. Smooth out the second layer as you did the first. The ends near the stems will not lie smoothly, of course, but don't worry; you'll take care of that when you wet out these areas.

At this point, I want to pause and give an alternative method of covering the outside of the hull. Often, in the interest of saving a little weight in the

45

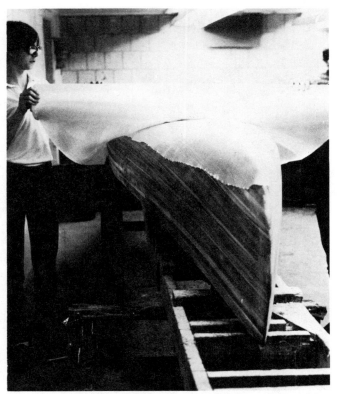

Rolling out the 60" cloth. The football-shaped bottom layer is already in place.

finished canoe, I don't make both outside layers *complete* layers. What I do is cut the first layer of cloth at about the waterline so that there is a football-shaped piece lying on the upside-down hull before the second, complete, covering is laid on. When the "football" is cut to shape, proceed as explained in the paragraph above. This method gives you the protection of a double layer of fiberglass on the bottom and at the heavy-wear areas near the ends where the canoe will get the most pounding and abrasion, and a single layer at the sides where hardly any damage is ever done. This option gives you a lot of extra fabric for other projects and does not lower the quality of the finished canoe, in my opinion. (Be sure to take the "football" from one side on the 60" fabric, not the middle!)

Now you are ready to start wetting out the fabric. Get your rollers, squeegees, and other tools ready, and mix up a batch of resin. For this first batch you should not have to even wet your roller(s). Just pour the resin on the bottom of the canoe and spread it with the squeegees. This method works anywhere you are working on a horizontal or near-horizontal surface. For the next batch of resin, mix and pour it into the roller pan and use the roller to wet out the sides of the canoe,

right down to the gunwales. The squeegees can be used here in conjunction with the rollers, but used alone, they make it hard to carry the resin to the cloth surface without losing some of it to the floor.

Except for the rollers used for carrying the resin to the sides of your canoe, your main tools for the wetting-out process are those handy little squeegees. Use them with enough pressure to force the resin into the fabric and remove the excess resin, but not enough to move the cloth. I have found that first-timers get the hang of this very quickly.

Continue wetting out the cloth, working toward the ends of the canoe. Be sure you do not leave any dry spots behind or between workers, and wet out completely to the gunwales before working toward the ends. Take care of any wrinkles or other trouble spots as they occur; don't leave them to be taken care of later. Do it now! You have ample time. The most common trouble ahead, as far as wrinkles are concerned, will be near the gunwale area. When a wave occurs there, do as I explained when you first spread out the cloth: walk to the stems and gently tug the wave out of the cloth before it becomes a wrinkle in the wetted cloth.

When you are within about a foot of the end of the canoe, you have to do something about bringing the fabric around the ends. Pause in your wetting out to prepare the end. The first thing that is

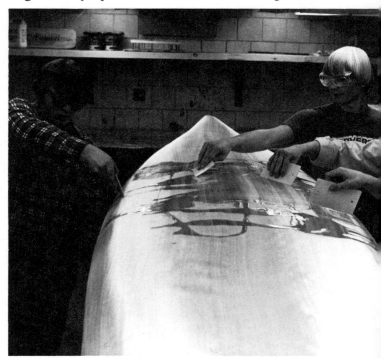

When wetting out the bottom, use the squeegees wherever possible.

46

The wetting out proceeds. The rollers are used to take the resin to the vertical surfaces, while the squeegees are used to even out the application on the horizontal and vertical portions.

obvious is that a slit must be cut nearly along the centerline of the cloth until it reaches the point where the cloth is in contact with the center of the canoe. However, *don't cut it exactly on center*. Make the cut about 1″ to 1½″ to one side. You'll see the wisdom in this when you wet it out and bring the cloth around the sharp end of the canoe. If the cut is made exactly in the center, the cloth will not behave and lie down where it is supposed to be.

Next, wet out one side completely to the end, but do not try to bring it around yet. If you are applying two complete layers, work with one layer at a time in this area. Just fold the top layer back out of the way until you get to it. Now cut off the side you just wetted out so that it follows the stem line of the canoe and reaches 2″ beyond it. A foam brush is handy now to carry resin to the hull and to assist in bringing the 2″ extension of cloth around the stem to the other side. Bring this extra cloth around and "tack" it in place with resin at about 6″ intervals along the stem line. This done, you should have a series of bulges between the places where you have "tacked" the cloth in place. Using brush, roller, and squeegee, you can make the cloth go into place around the stem without making a single slit in the cloth. A lot of resin helps; you can squeegee

off the excess later. Remember, you can push and pull the cloth a little to make it "stretch" into place. If you do have a lot of trouble with this technique, go ahead and make a slit or two. It will still come out all right.

Bring the other side of the cloth around the stem in the same manner. If you have two complete layers of fabric, continue with the other two, and then finish up the other end of your canoe. There will be some roughness at the cloth edge and where you made slits, if any, but these will be taken care of later when you sand in preparation for the finishing layers of resin.

When the wetting-out process is finished, the surface should have a matte finish; there should be no shiny spots indicating excess resin. If you see any such spots, use those squeegees to take care of the problem. The fabric is now completely saturated with resin, but the weave is only two-thirds filled. The filling is completed in subsequent coatings of resin. (See Figure 7.)

Now fuss around the still-wet hull for a while. Look carefully for white spots that indicate air pockets that have been trapped under the cloth.

Here's the slit that you will need at each end. It is about 1″ to 1½″ off center.

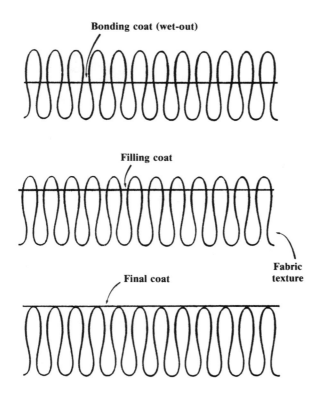

FIGURE 7 · Bonding and Filling Fiberglass Cloth

Use the squeegee and a little extra resin, if needed, to take care of them. It does no harm to work with the material right up to the point at which it hardens so much that you *can't* work with it. Keep your eyes on that gunwale area. The cloth likes to lift off there. However, don't get overly concerned if you miss one or two air pockets. They can be trimmed off later; and the gunwale strips cover that area, anyway.

In 15 or 20 hours you are ready to go to work again. Do the sanding with 80-grit sandpaper in an orbital sander. The only place that really requires much sanding is where you brought the cloth around the end. There you should carefully feather out the edge so it will be invisible when finish coats of resin are applied. The rest of the hull will only require a light sanding to remove irregularities and any dust that may have settled on the wet resin.

When the hull is completely sanded and wiped free of dust, you can apply a thin coat of resin with the rollers. Don't overdo it with resin here or you will get drips and runs. You'll soon get a feel for it. You are filling up the weave in the cloth, but you cannot do it all at once. Continue the sanding and filling until the weave of your cloth completely disappears. This should happen in two or three coats. Do what is needed, but not more.

When you have the weave completely filled, the hull will be a smooth, shiny, beautiful thing to behold. You'd like to leave it that way, but there's a problem: resin is affected by sunlight. If you are to have a clear finish and allow that beautiful wood to show through, then you have to give the resin some protection from ultraviolet rays. You do this by applying a varnish that is designed for this purpose. Don't do it now, though, because you will just scratch it up while you are working on the inside. Give the hull one final light sanding to prepare it for the varnish, and leave it until you are finished with the inside and the woodwork. Then it is time for the final finish and (for a while, anyway) you will have a brand-new canoe that is scratch-free and pretty enough to be a piece of furniture.

Summary of materials and tools needed to fiberglass the canoe hull using epoxy materials

(includes enough material to do the inside also):

Materials

Fiberglass fabric, 6-ounce, 60″ wide, three times the length of the canoe plus 1 yard

24 to 27 pounds (see text) of epoxy resin

Minimum order of Microfibers or colloidal silica

Minimum order of Filleting Blend (see text)

Clean sticks to stir resin

Plastic or papers to cover floor

Tools

Scissors

Old clothes

2 roller pans

2 roller frames

18 roller covers

2 squeegees

Optional Tools

Mini Pumps

2 34-ounce mixing pots

2 16-ounce mixing pots

12 pairs of disposable gloves

Minimum order of protective cream

Goggles

Trim the cloth on each side about 2" beyond the stem, then . . .

. . . bring it around and "tack" it in several places with a wet brush, then . . .

. . . after you have worked most of the bulges out with the wet brush, smooth it flat with the squeegee.

When the fabric is completely wetted out, the surface finish should be matte, not shiny.

Polyester Resin

Polyester resin has some advantages and some disadvantages when compared with epoxy resin, so before you read further about this material, I will try to give you some pros and cons of each as seen from my point of view and experience. If you are still undecided as to which material to go with, maybe this information will help.

First the advantages of polyester resin:

(1)   It is used more widely than epoxy and so is easier to find locally.

(2)   It is less expensive than epoxy — about one-half the price if you shop around, sometimes even better than that.

(3)   It is much easier to apply than epoxy with locally available tools (brushes, paint rollers).

(4)   It is much easier to work with because of reduced viscosity.

(5)   Cure time can be controlled by adjusting the amount of hardener used.

(6)   A variety of resins are available to yield a more (or less) flexible finished product.

As for the disadvantages of polyester resin (or, "Why Gil switched to epoxy"), they have to do with chemistry and performance. Chemistry is not my thing, but I am familiar with canoes and how they perform. It did not take more than one summer of using an epoxy-built strip canoe on Maine's wilderness rivers to know that my work was cut out for me in the coming winter — to become proficient in using epoxy resin, because it surpasses polyester resin in the following ways:

(1)   Polyester resin does not bond with the wood as well as epoxy does, and so there is a chance that delamination will occur in time.

(2)   Polyester resin is more brittle than epoxy and so there is less flex, and therefore more chance of a break, in the canoe.

(3)   Because of polyester resin's poor bonding, any small break in the fiberglass layer will allow water to enter the wood and cause rapid delamination.

(4)   The finished product is even more susceptible to the sun's rays than is epoxy, and the result is that it becomes even more brittle.

(5)   Polyester resin gives off extremely foul, obnoxious fumes while in use. (See the chapter on safety.)

(6)   The hardener (methyl ethyl ketone peroxide, or MEK peroxide) is extremely flammable, and can cause eye or skin burns.

I have always made sure these materials were handled with great respect, and have used them for years with my students without a serious incident.

The fiberglassing procedure for using polyester resin is just about the same as the steps I have laid out in the previous section on epoxy resin. In fact, this resin can be applied with the same tools as those used with epoxy, but it can also be applied with locally available paintbrushes and rollers. (This is not true of epoxy.) If you choose to use polyester, I am assuming that you will obtain it and the other materials and tools locally. The foam brushes I mentioned for used with epoxy will not work with polyester, except for a very short duration. The resin dissolves the adhesive that holds the foam together, and the thing soon falls apart. Most any bristle brush will work, but if the brush is of a man-made material, I suggest you try it before starting the project to make sure it won't melt away. I have not had this trouble with any brushes I have bought, however.

You may have trouble locating 60"-wide fiberglass. Sometimes the 38" width is more common. In this case, just buy six times the length of your canoe, plus two yards for waste and wraparound. Overlap the cloth at the centerline of the canoe, both outside and in. If you are going to use double cloth on the bottom only and not on the sides, you can buy only five times the length of the canoe. Further savings are possible on the inside with 38" cloth by putting the cloth right on the bottom and using trimmings from the outside to cover the 6" or so along the gunwales that the main cloth cannot reach. In this case, you can buy four times the length of the canoe.

There is a wide variation in polyester resins, and you should follow the manufacturer's directions for mixing very carefully. However, I have found that the curing times they list in their directions are sometimes way off. I would recommend that you mix up a half pint or so, and try it by wetting out a piece of scrap fiberglass cloth on a piece of scrap wood. Time it and see for yourself how long you will have to work before the stuff starts to gel. The time can be adjusted, somewhat, by a variation in the amount of hardener; but there are limits to this, so read the instructions.

When I was building with polyester, I bought

mine from a local boatbuilder who had the technical knowledge that I did not. The advantage of this was that I had fresh resin always available and someone handy who understood it. Look around — there are small boatshops all over that use fiberglass, and many of them will be happy to sell resin along with free advice. Three gallons of resin should be enough for a 16′ or 18′ canoe.

Mix your resin in small batches, especially at first, until you determine how long you have before the material starts to gel. A quart or even a little less is a good quantity for two people. Increase this amount as you gain experience.

Sealer Coat (Polyester): This first step in the fiberglassing process is done after the finished hull is all sanded and filled. Use the same procedure as that outlined for epoxy, except here you can use throwaway paintbrushes or paint rollers for application. Allow the resin to cure for about 24 hours, and then sand very lightly *by hand*. Just remove the fuzziness and dust particles. For some reason unknown to me, power sanding at this point causes the resin to ball up on the sandpaper and make a mess of the surface.

Stem Reinforcement (Polyester): Follow the directions in the epoxy section, using your choice of application tools.

Fiberglassing the Hull (Polyester): Again, follow the directions for epoxy. You will not have the problem with runs that I cautioned against for epoxy, but still, all you want to do is to wet out the cloth. When you are done, there should be a matte finish.

A short time after you finish the wetting-out process, the resin should start to gel. It will still be soft, but you can touch the surface without getting any on your finger. When this happens, mix up another batch of resin and apply another coat. Do this once more, if necessary, to finish filling the weave of the cloth. This one-session wetting out and filling is one advantage of the polyester, as far as application technique is concerned. If you do not do the filling this way (or if the resin does not gel up as quickly as expected), you will have to sand *thoroughly* between coats of resin. The reason for this is that a layer of wax comes to the surface as the stuff cures. If you wait, that waxy layer has to be completely sanded off before the next layer, or you will not get a satisfactory bond.

In any case, you will have those rough edges of

fiberglass where you brought the cloth around the stems to sand and feather out. When you do this, you will sand the whole hull in preparation for the varnish coat (or another filler coat, if you did not accomplish it as outlined above). As with the epoxy, leave the sanded hull as is until the canoe is completely finished, then apply a nice, shiny coat of high-quality protective varnish for that brand-new look.

Summary of materials and tools needed to fiberglass the canoe hull using polyester resin

(includes enough material to do the inside also):

Materials

Fiberglass fabric, 6-ounce, 60″ wide, three times the length of the canoe plus 1 yard, or appropriate length of narrower material (see text)

3 gallons of polyester resin with hardener

Clean sticks to stir resin

Plastic or papers to cover floor

Tools

Scissors

Old clothes

Goggles

6 or 8 number 10 cans to mix resin

6 or 10 inexpensive brushes 2″ or 3″ wide

Measuring devices for resin and hardener

12 pairs of disposable gloves

In Conclusion

That's about it! Whether you have chosen to work with epoxy or polyester, I hope this chapter has given you the confidence to go ahead with the process of fiberglassing, which people seem to feel is the most difficult, challenging, and (to some) intimidating of all the steps in building a strip canoe.

If you have absolutely no experience with fiberglassing, use a little resin on small experiments to build up your confidence. The reinforcing strips that you will apply to the canoe are a chance to try out the stuff on a small scale and gain experience. In the unlikely event that you mess something up, it will not be too much work to remove the mistake and start over.

The Inside

Finishing up and fiberglassing the inside of your hull is not very much different than doing the outside, but there are a few special problems to overcome. On the premise that you have already been through the finishing and fiberglassing of the outside of the hull and are ready to tackle the inside, I have focused this short chapter on the special problems that you may encounter at this stage.

You've had 24 hours or more of curing time to admire your work since you applied that last coat of resin to the outside, and it is time to go to work again. You can now take the hull off the stations, for it can support itself.

Start by pulling the nails out of the forms where you nailed them onto the strongback. Don't forget the nails in the stem forms — these are hard to get because of the confined space at this point, but get them out one way or another. If you simply toenailed the stem forms into the crosspieces, you will be able to lift them free by just prying up with a bar; the nails will pull free.

When all of the nails have been removed, the hull and forms can be lifted from the strongback, turned over, and placed on some sawhorses rightside up. Give the stations a push or tap with a hammer and they will fall over, if they haven't done so already. The stem forms come out less easily. Give them a couple of good sharp whacks with a hammer to loosen them, then hook the hammer claw under the bottom, with a block of wood as a fulcrum, and pry up. Don't worry, you won't damage the hull. You should be able to dislodge the forms without too much force, thanks to the masking tape that you put on before applying the strips.

Look at that inside — what a mess! You have ahead of you nearly the same job that you had on the outside of the hull. The only difference is that it is a little harder to get at the inside. You will use the same tools, the scraper and the Surform plane, except that now you will want a rounded Surform blade instead of a flat one, and you should custom-shape a scraper to do a good job on those concave curves of the hull's inside.

Take a scraper blade that is new, or at least isn't worn away with repeated sharpening. Reshape the blade to a nice arc, using as much of the blade as is available to do this. When the shape is to your satisfaction, resharpen, and you have a scraper without any sharp corners to dig in and cause troublesome gouges as you smooth up the inside of your canoe. An electric grinder is convenient for shaping your scraper, but a few minutes with a good file will do the trick just as well. You will want to use the file to sharpen in any case.

The hull will slide around now as you work on it, because it no longer has the heavy stations and strongback to anchor it in place. You can overcome this insecurity by having someone hold it for you, or by lodging one end against a wall. Work with the scraper and Surform until the glue is removed and the strips are somewhat even with each other. I am never as fussy with the inside as I am with the outside, but the surface must be reasonably smooth if the fiberglass is to lay on properly. A wavy surface is all right, but allow no strip corners or other sharp edges to remain. Anything that will let the cloth bridge across between two points, leaving a void beneath, should be removed.

When you have done as much as possible with the scraper and Surform, use the sander and number 36 paper. Don't get overly concerned with that section in the stem which defies reach with

Once the fiberglassed outside has cured, the hull is turned right-side up.

The stations are dislodged by tapping, then removed.

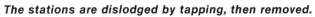

The stem form is more stubborn than the stations are, but firm, steady pressure with the hammer claw or a bar will pry it out.

The inside is smoothed up, using rounded-off scrapers . . .

. . . and a Surform.

54

practically any tool. Take a wood chisel and chip away and smooth up that area as well as you can, smooth it up by hand with sandpaper, and let it be.

Summary of materials and tools needed to finish the inside of the hull:

Materials
Number 36 sandpaper

Tools
Paint scraper
Surform plane with half-round blade
Flat file
Orbital sander

The Keel

If you wish to install a keel, this is the time to do it, before you fiberglass the inside. You will need a strip of ash or oak ¾″ × ¾″ wide and about 12′ long for a 16′ canoe. Measure the hull for the desired keel length, and cut the strip to fit. Taper and round off the ends to follow the line of the stems. Now turn the hull upside down and snap a chalkline to get the exact center (keel line) of the canoe. Mark where the ends of the keel will reach. Now drill a series of screw holes (shank size — 3/16″), along the centerline, with an electric or hand-powered drill. Make the first hole about 3″ from where the end of the keel will be and drill a hole every 6″. On the other end, split the difference on spacing to place your last hole 3″ from that end. Turn the hull over and countersink these holes on the inside of the canoe. Now, with the hull upside down again, carefully measure 3/8″ (half the thickness of the keel) to one side of your centerline of holes and make a series of marks. These marks will provide a visual reference against which to line up the keel as you screw it to the hull.

To attach the keel you'll need one person under the hull and one on top. You have to decide which job will be easier lying flat on your back, and which to do standing up. Holding the keel in place along the reference marks, drill a pilot hole with a 3/32″ drill, and drive home a screw (¾″ number 8 flathead). Put in the holes and screws as you go along; don't try to drill all your holes at once. If you work carefully and methodically, your keel will be straight.

Now, take out all of those screws and remove the keel. Take a piece of sandpaper and rough up the area on the hull where the keel is to lie. Mix some resin and apply it on the keel line and on the keel itself. It would be a good idea to mix in a little thickener, like colloidal silica, with the resin to be sure there are no voids between the hull and the keel. Replace the keel and secure it with screws. Clean up excess resin, and you now have a permanent waterproof joint.

Bilge keels are not used much anymore on canoes, but if you want them, just repeat the process as outlined for a single keel. Take care that they are exactly parallel to the main keel.

Summary of materials and tools needed to install the keel:

Materials
Ash or oak strip, ¾″ × ¾″, desired length
30 or more (depending on length of keel)
    ¾″ number 8 flathead brass screws
Resin, about a pint
Sandpaper
Foam brush for resin

Tools

3/32″ drill bit	Chalkline and chalk
3/16″ drill bit	Rule
Countersink	Pencil
Electric drill	Screwdriver

Fiberglassing the Inside

The experience you gained in fiberglassing the outside of your hull will stand you in good stead on the inside. The process is exactly the same, so I will only point out the aggravating little problems that may crop up and give some hints as to how to overcome them.

When you apply the sealer coat of resin, as well as when you are wetting out the cloth, any excess resin you apply will run to the bottom of the canoe, where it will collect in ever-thickening layers that, if allowed to harden, will give extra weight to lug around in the years to come. Also, the excess resin will float the cloth. (This situation will show up as waves in the wetted cloth's surface.) It does no harm, but adds excess weight, with no increase in strength. Watch for excess resin and keep it cleaned up; the place to watch most for this is near the stems. Those handy little plastic squeegees are your best tools for moving the resin out or to some place where it is needed.

When you are wetting out the cloth, watch for

Wetting out the inside layer of fiberglass cloth can be done entirely with squeegees.

but in fact it can be a little frustrating. The cloth that smoothed out so nicely over the convex hull on the outside will wrinkle up and fold on the inside. Start out in the middle and take care of the problems as they occur, smoothing out the cloth and gently tugging it into place as you apply the resin. Don't try to get everything absolutely smooth before starting to set out, but do get it in its approximate position. Then, as you go along, tease the cloth into place as you wet it out. Mix your resin in smaller batches so you don't have to worry about the stuff curing before you are ready. Go ahead and get started. Don't worry, you can do it.

The materials and tools needed to fiberglass the inside have been included with those for the outside to avoid confusion, so they are not repeated here.

bridging along the bilge area of the hull where the curve is the sharpest. I find that I am constantly adjusting the cloth with one hand along the gunwale while I am wetting out with the other.

When you get to each stem, don't try to bring the cloth around as you did on the outside. This is a very difficult place to work. Just cut the cloth an inch or two short of the point of the stem and wet it out. Continue wetting into the point with resin to be sure the wood there is well sealed. I used to bring the cloth around the point inside, but it is an exasperating chore, and I found that eliminating it resulted in a neater job with no sacrifice in strength or quality of the finished canoe. An excessive amount of resin must be used to properly seal this area, so be prepared to clean up the run-off that will collect at the bottom if you don't want a half-inch or so of extra thickness there.

My final bit of advice for fiberglassing the inside is to have patience. I wish I could say it is a snap,

Finishing up the ends. A foam brush is a good tool here.

The Woodwork

I have watched a lot of capsized canoes suffer the indignity of being swamped and finding their own way — bumping, grinding, and scraping over rocks and ledges — as they got through the rapids (if the owners were lucky) to quieter water, where they slowed up and waited to be recovered. The canoes that have survived this ordeal relatively unscathed were not necessarily those with super-rugged hulls, but rather, those with a strong, well-put-together framework — the woodwork, mainly the gunwales and thwarts. Without the rigidity of this framework, the canoe, any canoe, is subject to twisting, racking, and bending. Most hulls do not withstand this kind of treatment very well.

The woodwork for your canoe consists of four parts: the gunwales (or rails), the decks, the thwarts and/or yoke, and the seats. Only the first three will be discussed in this chapter; the seats are a separate project described in a later chapter. (You might leave this book lying around, open to the seat chapter, where your spouse can see it. She or he might take the hint and start making and caning them so they'll be ready when the rest of the woodwork is done.)

Canoe makers use a wide variety of woods for the woodwork. It depends on what part of the country they live in, their own personal preference, and the intended purpose of the canoe. Probably the most common wood found in Maine is white ash, and this is my choice for the woodwork. White ash is strong, bends well, and is relatively light. Oak is sometimes used. It is as strong as, if not stronger than, ash; it is a little heavier, though. Other hardwoods — maple, birch, mahogany — have been used, and these serve their purpose well. Mahogany is an exotic, and I'm not sure if it fits the hardwood category as we know it here, but it is used extensively. Spruce is a popular wood for gunwales, because of its high strength-to-weight ratio. However, it is rather soft and does not stand up well to the abrasion of sliding on and off a roof rack of a car. This is a shortcoming of mahogany as well.

You will quickly discover that the problem isn't what kind of hardwood to use for your gunwales, but where to find stock that is long enough. Through my years of searching, I have convinced local woodsmen and sawmill operators that I need this long material, and so a few long boards come my way each year, but there never seems to be an overabundance of them. The most reliable source for long ash (or other hardwood) is any sawmill located where there is a lot of shipbuilding or boat-building going on. In these areas, the sawmills cater to boatbuilders by sawing long logs to provide the lengths they need. You will very seldom find the long material you need in a lumberyard that serves builders and home owners, although this is a good place to start your search; your local yard will know what is going on in the industry.

For the yoke and thwarts, use a strong hardwood like ash. These, like the seats, are subjected to all kind of stress, and you need their strength as cross-braces. I often find myself stepping on them when I am climbing over the gear of my loaded canoe when going ashore. If they are not strong enough for this treatment, they aren't strong enough.

For the decks I have used a wide variety of woods depending on availability, my whims, and purpose of the canoe. Since ash is the wood — except for cedar — the most available to me, that is what I use most often. (I have used cedar, too, when I wanted to trim ounces off the finished weight of the canoe, but usually I'm not that wor-

Clamping up the gunwales.

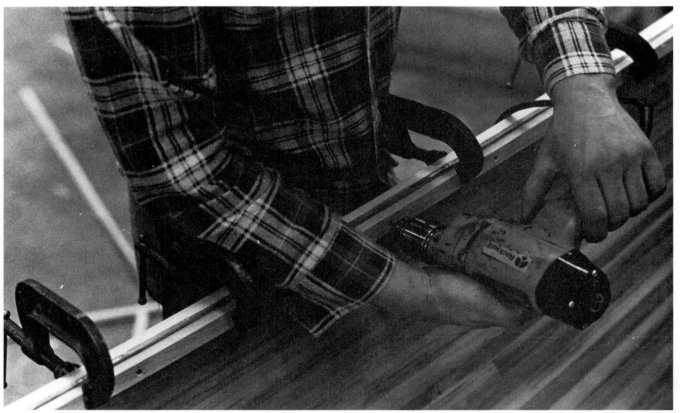

Drilling the pilot holes.

ried about weight.)

For hardware, I use brass. This is sometimes hard to find and always more expensive, but I feel it is worth it. If your local hardware stores cannot get brass for you, try a marine supplier. Almost any dealer who handles screws, bolts, nuts, and other fastenings has sources for brass hardware, but many dealers are unwilling to go to the trouble of making special orders for their customers. You do not *have* to use brass, however; I use it for reasons of aesthetics and quality. Regular plated-steel screws and bolts will serve just as well, and stainless steel, galvanized, and other types of fastenings are commonly used by boatbuilders. (Check Appendix I at the end of this book for some sources of hardware supplies.)

Wherever you need waterproof glue — and that includes the decks — resin is the best there is. Just add a little thickener to the mixed resin. It will bond the parts permanently together and act as a filler for those places where you might not have succeeded in a perfectly close fit.

The Gunwales

The gunwales, or rails, serve as the foundation for the rest of the woodwork, and so they are the first to be installed. They don't require much material in terms of board feet, but as I said before, they do have to be long. As a last resort you can make a long splice in the gunwale strips to attain the length you need, but this will be a weak spot in your framework. If you have to resort to this, use epoxy glue and stagger your joints — that is, do not let the splice on an inside gunwale be opposite that of the outside one. The screws that hold the inside and outside gunwales together, can be placed so as to assist in holding the joints more securely together.

The gunwale strips should be ¾" by ¾" for the outside ones, and 3/8" by ¾" for the inside. Inside gunwales can also be ¾" by ¾" if you wish. I use these thicker inwales on big canoes. Start with a 1" board, 4" or 5" wide and *at least* 6" longer than your canoe. One extra foot in length will give you a little insurance. Measure carefully along the sheerline of your canoe to determine how much leeway you think you'll need. I buy my boards in the rough, so the first thing I have to do is plane the board to ¾" thickness. Now, every strip I take off with the table saw will be ¾" in one dimension by whatever I set the saw fence to take off — in this case, two ¾" strips and two 3/8" strips. If the board you are using is clear and free

of knots, you will have some wood left over when these four strips are sawn off, maybe enough for another canoe. If you do have a remaining piece of this valuable long wood, I suggest you save it for future use rather than cut it up for the rest of your woodwork. The shorter pieces are not hard to find or expensive to buy.

To install the gunwale strips on the hull, start by holding the inwale strip where it is to go and trim it to length. A couple of inches short of the stem on each end will be ok; look ahead to the section on decks to see what I mean. Now, while holding it in place, make a mark right in the center of the strip. (The center of the canoe is located at the row of staple holes where the center station was located.) Using this strip for a pattern, trim the other one to length and mark the center. Measure in each direction from the center, making a mark every 6". These marks indicate the positions of the screws that will hold the gunwales in place.

If you have purchased a combination drill-countersink (some are sold under the trade name of Screw-Mate), you can proceed as described in the following paragraph. If you are drilling pilot holes and shank holes and countersinking in separate operations, you should drill the shank holes and countersink the inwales before clamping them in place on the canoe. It is easier this way on a drill press, if you have one, or on a bench with a hand-held drill. When the gunwale strips are clamped in place, all you will have to drill is the pilot hole for the screw threads.

Starting at the center of the canoe, use C-clamps to hold the gunwale strips along the sheerline. I like to leave 1/16" to 1/8" of the edge of the hull above the level of the hardwood strips to ensure a nice, level surface when the top surface of the gunwale is smoothed up. Position the clamps between the marks where you have to drill (or the holes you *have* drilled), so that you'll have room to use the drill and a screwdriver. You probably should have six or eight C-clamps for this operation; more would be better if you can get your hands on them. Where the sheerline is fairly flat, one clamp between every other mark should be sufficient; where the line curves, you will need a clamp between every mark. Use as many clamps as you have. Keep the strips even with each other and slightly below the top of the sheerline. When you run out of clamps, put in your screws, remove the clamps, and do another section of your rails. Keep doing this until you reach the end.

To fasten the gunwales you will need 1¼",

Driving the screws.

number 8, flathead screws. It will take 65 or 70 screws for a 16-footer. When the holes have been drilled, by whatever method you chose, tighten the screws into place. You will almost certainly need to apply some form of lubrication to the threads of the screws in order to turn them into the hardwood. The handiest lubricant for this purpose is a slightly moistened piece of soap. Just scrape the threads across the bar, and enough soap will be deposited to ensure good lubrication. If it is still tough going and the screw resists being wound all the way home, check the depth of your pilot hole. When using brass, it is especially important not to force the screw if it resists your efforts. The metal is soft, and the screw is easily twisted off.

Again, look ahead to the deck section. The fitting of your decks will determine where the last screw will have to be located near the ends of each gunwale. It is possible that you will not have to use the last mark or hole you made on the inwale, but this depends on where it ended up on your canoe.

When the gunwale strips are all in place, you may want to dress down the top of the gunwales, bringing the top edge of the fiberglass and cedar strips to the level of the hardwood gunwale strips. This will lessen the chance of your cutting yourself on the sharp fiberglass edges as well as make the canoe a little easier to handle. Use a Surform or whatever power or hand tool you have on hand that will do the job. This done, you are ready to proceed to the decks.

The Decks

I have included here two possible methods for making decks — the cap deck and the flush deck. A quick look at the photos will make their differences apparent. I, and most of my students, prefer the flush deck. It is made of less (or narrower) wood and looks a bit more professional when finished, I think. The cap deck is a little easier to install and will serve to cover up if a serious mistake was made somewhere on the end. Whichever style deck you choose, a good job of hand-fitting each individual deck will ensure a good-looking job.

The Cap Deck: Width for it is not critical, but the narrower it is, the shorter it will be. Your canoe shape will affect this, too. The board should be at least ¾ " thick — though I prefer 7/8 ", or even 1 " thickness, if possible. When you decide the length you want, you can determine how wide a board you'll need. Supposing you want the bow deck to be 12 " wide, you can, if necessary, glue and dowel two pieces of wood together to attain this width. When ready, lay your board in position and trace along the outwale strip on each side. Cut along this line to end up with a triangular piece. Duplicate this procedure for the stern deck.

Cap decks, ready to install.

Now, cut a rabbet in the triangular pieces to fit the gunwales. (I make the rabbet deep enough so that there is ½ " of wood above the gunwales.) It usually takes some fitting before the deck will lie flat, making proper contact with the tops of the gunwales. Do this individual fitting for each end for a good craftsmanlike fit. For a graceful touch, give the edge of the deck (toward the center of the canoe) a nice curve. (Look at the photos.)

Now you are ready to install the decks. Make a line for the screw holes on the deck over each inwale. Use six or eight screws for each deck, giving them a nice, even spacing. Drill and countersink your shank holes in the deck (unless you are using a combination bit). Apply epoxy or waterproof glue between the deck and the gunwales, and clamp the deck in place as shown in the photos. Now drill the pilot holes for your screws, or make complete holes if you are using a combination bit. Wind the lubricated screws into place and leave everything as is until the glue is cured. The screws for these decks should be 1 ", number 8, flathead. If you use the

longer, 1¼ " screws, left over from the gunwales, they will probably come through the bottom of the inwale, but these ends can be filed off and do no harm. You will need 12 or 16 screws, depending on how many you decide to use for each end.

When the glue is ready to be worked, the clamps can be removed and you can proceed to round off the edges of the decks and gunwales to suit your own taste. At this point I recommend that you continue with the sanding and complete the finishing of the decks and gunwales (short of varnishing) at this time, as it is easier now than when the thwarts and yoke have been attached. Seats and thwarts are sanded separately. Drill a hole in each deck so that you can attach a rope (painter) to the ends of the canoe (unless you plan to install a ring for this purpose), and you are ready to proceed to the next step.

The Flush Deck: You will not need as wide a piece of wood for this style as for the cap deck, but the thickness should still be ¾ " to 1 "; I usually prefer the middle thickness, or 7/8 ". A 6 " board around 2 ' in length will be sufficient for making both flush decks. Here is a good place to add a personal touch with an exotic wood or some fancy-grained hardwood that you have been saving for just the right purpose.

Especially if you are using a special piece of wood, I recommend that rather than tracing directly from your canoe onto the deck material, you first make a cardboard pattern and shape it until it fits; then use this to cut out the decks. Once you determine the angle, the sides of the pattern can be straightened out with a straightedge, even though the sides of the canoe are not ruler-straight. Later, when you screw the decks in place, the flexible canoe will pull in to close any gaps. The reason for the pattern is that it is difficult to get a true line from the rather rough surface of the sheerline; also, the inwale is in the way for part of the line you have to make. When you are satisfied with the pattern, cut out the decks. They do not yet have the notches for the inwales that appear in the photo; you will make these notches next. Lay the decks in place on top of the inwales to ensure a perfect fit. You may want to use a fine rasp to smooth up the inside of the canoe where the fiberglass may be a little rough; this will give you a finer line with no gaps where the deck meets the sides of the canoe.

Next, decide how far you want the inwales to extend into the deck; I usually plan on at least 2½ " to 3 ". With this established, cut all inwales to the same length. The best method of establishing a line that is equal for all four inwales is to measure from

Cap decks — glued, clamped, and then screwed into place.

Finished cap deck, ready for finish.

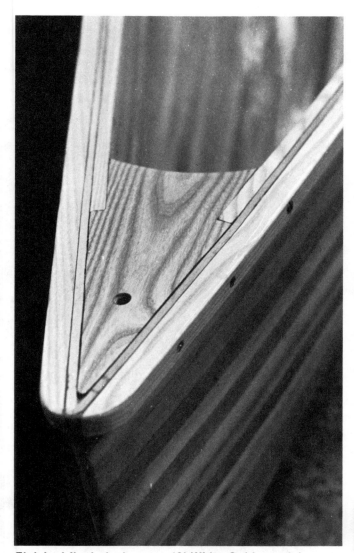

Finished flush deck on an 18' White Guide model.

the point of the stem, using an equal distance for all of them. Cut the inwales off square for a nice fit into the deck. This is a rather cramped place to use a regular handsaw. If you have (or have access to) a sabersaw, you will find this to be the best tool for the job. Otherwise, a keyhole saw is a good choice. Whatever saw you use, be careful not to cut into the side of your canoe.

Once you have established that the flush deck will fit tightly into the canoe when the notches for the inwales have been cut, lay the deck pieces on the canoe and very carefully mark around the ends of the inwales onto the underside of the decks. An extra set of hands is helpful here for holding the decks in place while you make the necessary marks. *It is important that these marks be accurate to ensure a good fit.* Draw your lines, and cut the notch-

es. I always caution my students to stay slightly off the line, leaving a little extra wood on the decks for final fitting. You can always take a little more off, but you can't put it back on.

Fit the decks individually. A helpful hint for achieving a good fit between the deck and the canoe, and a trick of all finish carpenters, is to take a little more wood from the bottom of the deck, where it doesn't show, rather than from the top. In other words, taper the edges slightly from top to bottom. This way, minor adjustments are easier to make, and any roughness in the canoe that might interfere with the two pieces coming together evenly, with a nice fine line, are neutralized.

When you are satisfied with the fit, establish the locations of the screw holes, drill the shank holes in the gunwales, and countersink them. You will want one screw through both gunwales where the inwale extends into the notch. These screws will need to be at least 2″ long. The other screws (two more for each side are usually enough) can be 1½″ long. When the shank holes are ready, make up some epoxy or waterproof glue and prepare to screw the decks in place.

Here again, the extra hands are helpful. Apply the glue to both surfaces to be joined. It is a good idea to put some paper inside the canoe to protect it from any dripping glue. When you are ready, have someone hold the deck in place and drill one of the pilot holes for a screw. Put in the screw im-

Flush deck, ready to install.

Drilling pilot holes into the flush deck. Glue is already in place.

Here is another idea for a deck. For something different on the modified Wabnaki, I installed a hardwood crosspiece and then filled in the triangle with cedar strips in a pattern similar to the bottom of the canoe. The strips were 3/8" thick.

Sanding the gunwales.

mediately; it will help hold the deck in place while you drill for and fasten the other screws. Continue until all of the screws are in place. While fastening the deck, strive to keep its surface as even with that of the top of the gunwales as possible. (I called it a flush deck, remember?) The more even you can get it now, the less dressing down you will have to do when the glue is cured. That's what comes next.

Making everything flush and even on the ends is best accomplished with a power sander that is capable of removing a lot of wood rather fast. Perfect alignment here seldom happens, and this may be where you are glad you have a little extra thickness in the deck piece. A belt sander with a coarse belt is good for this; so is a disc sander with a coarse disc. Of course, hand tools will do the job with a little more time and elbow grease. However you do it, get the surface of deck, the canoe (edge of the top strip), and the gunwales nice and even and level with each other. The glue will have filled in any unavoidable gaps, and the evened-off deck will look better than you thought it would when you screwed it together. When the surface is complete, proceed to round off the gunwales and bring the decks and the gunwales to the varnishing stage. You will hold off on that, however, until you have installed thwarts and/or yoke.

The Thwarts

Canoes that are 16' in length or shorter have only one thwart in the center, although you can install more if you wish. For this single thwart in 16-footers, and for the center thwart in longer canoes, I use the yoke as shown in the photos and in Figure 8. However, suit yourself as to the shape you like for this purpose. The longer canoes should have three thwarts. Make them as fancy or as plain as you wish. You can custom-shape your yoke to fit you by modifying the pattern, or you can use this pattern as is.

The yoke I use, and the one patterned here, is not intended for long portages. It is for the short haul from car to water, etc. When carrying the canoe over long distances, I always tie my paddles in place on the yoke so that the canoe rests directly on my shoulders *through them*. A padding made from my life preserver completes the portage outfit. If one is to make a yoke large enough to be comfortable over a long portage, it will have to be much wider than mine, and therefore a lot heavier. I don't like to carry extra weight around day after day just for the occasional use of a heavy-duty yoke; my paddles go with me, anyway.

For your yoke and thwarts, use a hardwood board ¾" thick. For the yoke, the wood will need to be about 5" wide. For the thwarts, a 2" width will do. Cut the pieces a little longer than needed at this point; you will trim them to fit later. When you have cut them to shape, round off the edges to your satisfaction and proceed to sand and finish them. Varnish them, too, if you wish, though this can be done when you finish the rest of the canoe.

You have a little choice at this point as to the final width of the canoe. You can either widen it or pull it in a bit. Usually it is best to go with the established width, unless you have a special reason for doing otherwise. If you don't remember the designed width, get out the center station and measure it at the sheerline. This measurement is the width of the inside of your canoe. You can safely cut the yoke off at that length. Remember, you want the yoke to be perfectly centered across the canoe, so take off an equal amount from each end. Don't depend on the hull to have maintained the correct width; it could have curled in or sagged out a little since you removed it from the stations.

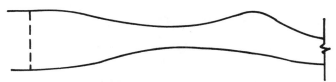

FIGURE 8 · Outline for Yoke

Install the yoke and thwarts under the inwale strip by drilling with a 3/16" drill bit down through the gunwale strip and through the thwart or yoke. Countersink the hole and install the machine bolt. When you drill, you may want to angle the drill slightly so that the hole enters the thwart or yoke not too close to its end. Use two 10-32 or 10-24 flathead machine screws, 2" long, for each end of the yoke and one on each end of the other thwarts. The center thwart or yoke can be placed in the exact center of the canoe as established by the center row of staple holes, or you can establish the balance point of the canoe. If you choose to establish the balance point, it will have to be put off until everything else, including the seats, have been installed. I have found that the exact center is almost always a comfortable balance — slightly light in the front, the way I like it.

When the center thwart or yoke is installed, you are done if the length is 16' or shorter, but for the

Installing the yoke.

longer models there are still two more. For 18′ to 20′ canoes, I place the other two thwarts about 42″ to 44″ from the center one. This distance is not a hard-and-fast rule, and you can modify it to suit yourself.

When all of the thwarts are in place, you can proceed with the varnishing of the canoe and the woodwork, because the seats are varnished before being caned. You will want to put at least two coats of marine-quality varnish on the fiberglass portion of the canoe and three coats on the woodwork. Select a varnish that filters out ultraviolet rays.

66

You might want to leave the final coat until the seats are installed just to be sure to cover up every last scratch.

If your hint was taken and a pair of nicely caned seats are waiting for you, just skip to the end of the seat chapter and install them according to the directions there. Otherwise, continue on — the seats aren't as complicated as they may look. And if the ice is out and you don't see how you are going to wait to get those seats caned, cheer up! There *is* a way to hurry things. Read on to the first part of the next chapter.

Summary of materials and tools needed to complete the woodwork
(quantities will vary with canoe length and style of decks used):

Materials

Hardwood board, ¾" thick, 4" or 5" wide, 6" to 12" longer than the canoe

Hardwood board, ¾" or 7/8" thick, 11" or 12" wide, 30" long, for the cap decks *or*,

Hardwood board, ¾" or 7/8" thick, 6" wide, 24" long for flush decks

Hardwood board, ¾" thick, 5" wide, 36" long for the yoke

2 hardwood boards, ¾" thick, 30" long for thwarts (if canoe is longer than 16')

86 brass screws, 1¼" or 1½", number 8, flathead

4 to 8 (depending on canoe length), flathead machine screws, 10-32 or 10-24, 2" long, with nuts

4 brass screws, number 8 or 10, 2", flathead

8 brass screws, number 8, 1½", flathead

Hand soap for screw threads

Waterproof glue or epoxy glue

3 or 4 sheets of 50-grit sandpaper

2 or 3 sheets of 100-grit sandpaper

Fine steel wool

2 quarts of marine-quality varnish with UV (ultraviolet) filter

Tools

Table saw

Electric hand drill

Bandsaw or sabersaw

Orbital sander

Rule

Handsaw

Surform plane with flat blade

6 or more C-clamps

Screwdriver

Countersink

5/16" drill bit

3/16" drill bit

Combination drill bit to make countersunk holes for 1¼" number 8 flathead screws

1 or 2 varnish brushes

Seats

In his book *Maine Lingo*, Maine humorist John Gould gives the following regional interpretation of an otherwise common English word:

Ample — Favored Maine word to express satisfaction at table:
"Have more potatoes, Cyrus?"
"No, thanks Helen, *ample* of everything."
A time-tested dialogue as old as Maine is between a deaf hostess and her gentleman guest. She speaks first:
More vegetables, Jonathan?
No, thanks — great sufficiency.
Been a-fishin'?
No, I say — I've got plenty!
Caught twenty?
No, no — I'm full!
Broke your pole?
No, no — *ample, ample*!
Small sample — pass up your plate![1]

In my section of Maine the word was also used, especially by my grandparents' generation, to describe something as being large enough that its size could be put out of mind for once and for all.

"That crock big enough, Ben?"
"*Ample,* Gertie, *ample.*"

The reason for this bit of northern New England humor is simply so that you will know what I mean when I describe my canoe seats as *ample*. They are big enough so a person can spend the day on one of them and have room to squirm, wiggle, and shift to stay comfortable. Furthermore, the plastic cane used has enough stretch and ventilation to make the above contortions all but unnecessary. Never do I feel the irresistible desire to stand and rub my posterior to restore circulation. Since most of my summer days are spent in the stern of a canoe, I value this bit of comfort, and so I do not skimp on

the seats. It takes only a little extra care to make a first-class seat. I can't for the life of me understand why some canoe builders insist on putting in seats that are little better to sit on than a thwart!

(Most canoe-builders would figure that the term "beamy" refers to the width of a boat. However, this term, too, is carried a bit further in Maine, and in *Maine Lingo* the definition is finished up with the following: "*Beamy* is a favorite Maine adjective for a lady with steatopygous accumulation." The lady would be comfortable on my seats.)

Making the Frames

Look at Figure 9. You will see designs for two styles of canoe seats. Each drawing shows, superimposed, both the bow seat and the stern seat (length shown with broken lines). All of the dimensions you will need to cut and lay out your seats are given. The horizontal pieces are long enough to fit any canoe you might build; they are designed to be trimmed to fit. Most of my students, and myself, prefer the top (tapered) design because the side (vertical) pieces follow the lines of the canoe and result in a more professional-looking job. Besides, the tapered seats allow more room.

All stock should be ash or some other hardwood, and should measure ¾ " by 1½ ". (Sometimes if my stock has some small knots that I think might prove to be weak spots in the seat frames, I will use up to 2 " stock for added strength, but this also adds weight.) When you have your hardwood to size, cut the lengths you will need. You will have eight pieces for your pair of seats. If you decide to use lap joints, you should make the vertical pieces a little longer than the indicated 15 " to allow for trimming and for the slight angle. For other types of joints, that length will be more than *ample*.

---

[1] John Gould, *Maine Lingo* (Camden, Maine: Down East Books, 1975), p.35.

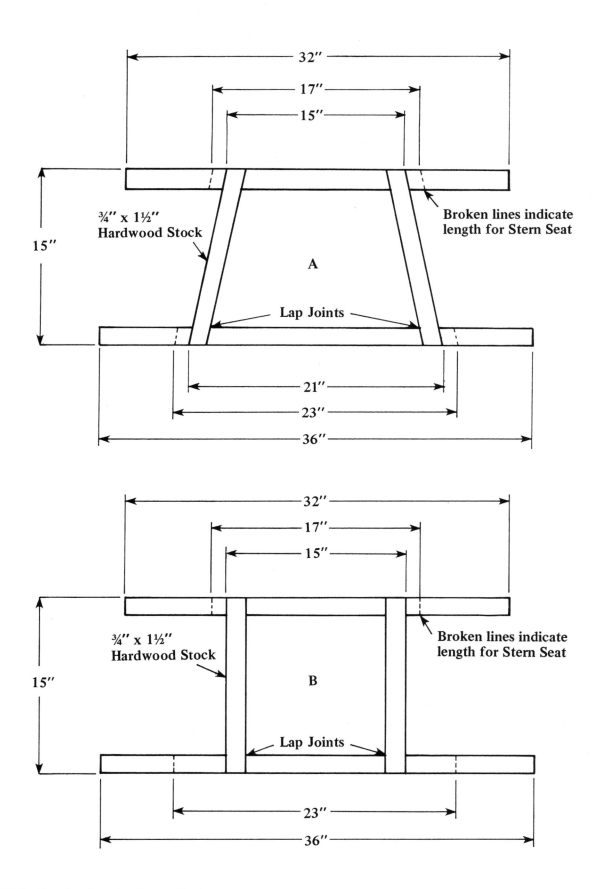

FIGURE 9 · Two Designs for Canoe Seats

Figures 10, 11, and 12 show the three best choices for wood joints for this type of project. Of these, the strongest is the mortise-and-tenon joint. In compliance with Murphy's Law, it is also the hardest to make. However, I feel it is worth the trouble, so it is what I and my students use. This joint was used by wood joiners long before the first power tool was thought of, so it can be made using even the simplest of hand tools. My second choice is the doweled joint. I think Murphy slipped up here, because this joint seems, to me, easier to make than the weakest of the three, which is the lap joint. I used to use the lap joint, but I found that it weakened the wood and, unless I went to larger pieces of stock, these joints often broke after a season or so of use, even if they hadn't carried a real heavyweight.

Here's the easiest way to make the angled seats shown in the top drawing. When you have your stock cut to length, lay out the two horizontal pieces 15″ apart and parallel, as shown. Next, lay the vertical pieces on top of them, crossing at the points indicated (21″ apart for the edge nearest you, 15″ for the top). Now, by carefully working with a sharp pencil, establish and mark the points and angles where they cross each other. (If you opt for the square seats shown in the bottom drawing, most of the marking can be done with a rule and square, since there are no angles to contend with.)

Now cut the joints for whatever type you have chosen. (If you are new to this, refer to any manual on basic woodworking skills.) When you are satisfied with their fit, they should be put together with a good waterproof glue. If you are using WEST SYSTEM resin for your canoe, just mix a small amount of this with some thickener until you have a glue-like consistency, and apply it. (Other than the resin, I have found the best glue to be the two-part variety marketed in two cans, usually taped together. One can contains liquid, the other a powder. I have repaired paddle blades with this stuff, and they have withstood seasons of use. Several companies market it; I have found no differences in them.) For the mortise-and-tenon joint or the doweled joint, the glue is all you need. With the lap joint, you should use two wood screws at each corner to help reinforce the glue.

If you have four bar clamps, these are the most convenient tools for holding the seat parts together until the glue sets. However, these glues do not require a lot of pressure; so if you do not have access to clamps, just lay the seat frames on a flat surface that you do not mind driving a few nails into. Put

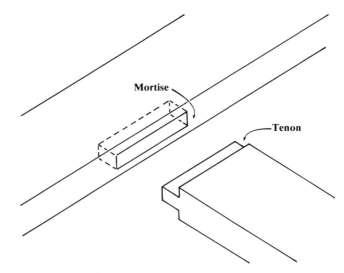

FIGURE 10 · Mortise-and-Tenon Joint

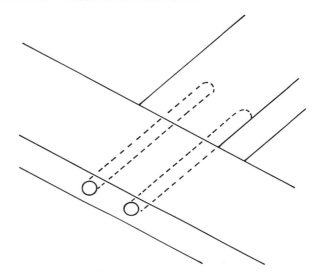

FIGURE 11 · Doweled Joint

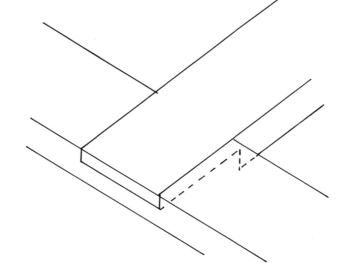

FIGURE 12 · Lap Joint

Laying out the seat angles.

scrap boards against the front and rear, forcing them together by hand as you do so. Now just drive a nail into the scrap pieces to hold everything in place until the glue has hardened. (You'd probably better put some plastic or something between the seat frame and your work surface to prevent them from sticking together.)

When the frames are together and you are ready to proceed, smooth up the joints a little, removing excess glue and making things level and true before you mark the holes for caning. Delay most of your sanding, though, until the holes are drilled.

The holes should be on a line drawn 3/8″ from the inside edge of the frame. Make this line on all four sides of your frame. The crossing of the lines at the corners establishes the locations of your corner holes for the caning operation. Now find the center of *each* of the four sides of your seat, and

space your holes ¾″ in each direction from the center mark. As you approach the corner, it becomes obvious that the distance from the last hole you'll mark and the corner hole will not necessarily be ¾″. Use your judgment here; you can usually split the difference and make the last couple of holes either a little closer or a little farther apart than ¾″. However, since you started in the center, make sure that whatever adjustment you make on one end of the side, is duplicated on the other end. Once you have marked all four sides of both seats, you are ready to start drilling. You will need a ¼″ drill bit and the means of turning it.

The holes are easiest to drill with a drill press, but a power hand drill will do fine if you are careful to keep it perpendicular to the surface for each hole so you don't go through at an angle. A hand drill will do the job, if necessary.

71

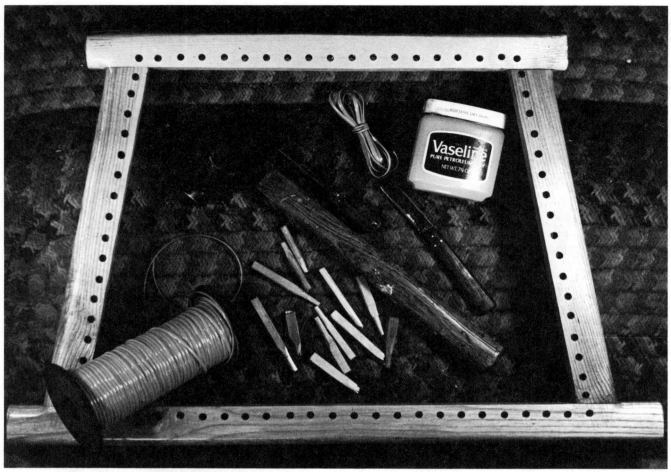

The tools and makin's of a caned canoe seat.

I like to round off the outside edges of the seats for comfort and good looks. This can be done with a router with a rounding cutter, or simply with a wood rasp, until the desired contour is reached. Now sand the frame until it meets your standards. Finally, two or three coats of the high-quality marine varnish you used for your canoe should be applied to the frames. When this is dry, you are ready to start caning. If you would rather use natural cane instead of the recommended plastic cane, delay the application of the varnish until the caning is completed, then give the seat frame *and* the cane several coats.

Caning

One of my adult students was a shop teacher in another school system and had experience in caning chair seats with natural cane. In a discussion of the subject, he remarked that he was going to use the real thing for his canoe seats. I asked him why. He said that he liked the idea of using traditional materials, the modern plastic seeming somehow

out of place. I laughed and pointed out that he was using space-age materials to build his canoe, even though the finished product *did* have a natural appearance, and yet he wanted traditional seats. He laughed along with me and said that I was right, but I suspect that he used the natural material anyway.

Natural cane has one major disadvantage that, as far as I am concerned, makes it unsuitable for canoe seats: it stretches and sags in damp weather (there is always plenty of *that* on a canoe trip), and then it does not return to its original shape when dry. The plastic cane always remains taut and flexible, bounces back from the roughest treatment, and seems to be unaffected by heat or cold. I have plastic-caned canoe seats that have been in use for so long, I'm beginning to think the cane will outlast the wooden frame it is strung upon.

If you have prepared for the caning operation, you should already have the necessary tools and materials to complete this phase of the seat project. The photo above shows the tools and materials you will need for weaving plastic cane, and I will explain the purpose of each item as we get to it. If you are using natural cane, the only extra thing you need is a container of water in which to soak and soften the cane. As for plastic cane, I hope you are lucky enough to buy yours on a nice, neat spool like the one shown. It is often sold in hanks, and it is more of a chore to pull each piece out.

Get comfortable, and we'll get to work. I will be referring to the back and front of the seat from time to time, so let's establish which is which: While caning, we'll consider the wide part of the seat (closest to you) the front, and the narrow part the back. The two angled pieces in the photos will be called the sides. (If your seat is of a different design, just establish in your mind which is which and follow along; it makes no difference what the shape is.) You may want to work with the seat in your lap, but I like to set up two chairs and suspend the seat between them so I can get at the top and bottom as I work. Some of my students clamp the seat to the edge of a table so it is held securely for

them. You will quickly establish what works best for you.

Step 1: Start out by counting the holes in the front and back to find the center hole of each, which you then mark with a peg. As long as the two marked holes are opposite each other, all will be well. Get out a convenient length of cane. For these early steps I use 16′ to 18′ lengths. Later, when the weaving begins, I shorten the lengths somewhat so as not to have so much material to pull through. (Use your arms as a convenient measure. Most people can reach roughly their own height with their arms outstretched, so if you are a 6-footer, you'll measure 6′ of material to a stretch.)

Start in the rear center hole and string the cane across to the front center hole. Notice that the cane has a right side and a wrong side. The rounded side should be up; you will have to keep it that way throughout the project. Be sure to leave 4″ or 5″ of cane hanging below the seat wherever there is an end so that you will have something to get hold of when you tie off later. You will go down through

Step 1, half-finished. Just fill in the other side.

the front center hole and come up through the one to its right. Go across toward the rear and go down through the hole to the right of the rear center hole. Continue this stringing until the side is filled. I like to follow along with a peg to hold the cane taut in each hole until I pull the next one tight, then move the peg along. Do not try to pull the cane really tight, but just tight enough to keep the strands straight and in place. Things will tighten up later when you begin to weave.

When you approach the angled sides, just keep the shorter strands parallel with the others by moving from hole to hole along the angled pieces. (Check photo on page 73.) The shorter strands on each side will have to be pegged on both ends so that the cane will not be strung across the holes underneath the seat. When you have filled in the right side of the seat, string up the other side in the same manner. This completes Step 1.

Step 2: Start this step by pegging off the end of your strand in the hole next to the right rear corner. (See photo below.) Go across the seat horizontally to the corresponding hole on the other side. You are stringing these strands right across those put on in Step 1. Continue stringing horizontally across your seat until it is filled from rear to front. Don't worry about all those untied strands hanging below the seat; we'll get to them shortly.

Step 3: So far, things are easy. (Don't worry — they aren't going to get much more complicated, either.) This step is a repetition of Step 1. Start in a hole on one side or the other of the one you started with in Step 1, and string a new vertical layer of cane right over the layers put on in Steps 1 and 2. You'll end up with three layers of cane. The photo on page 75 shows the right side of the seat with this step completed; I tried to push the strands apart so you could see the three layers. When you have filled in both sides of the seat, turn the seat over, and we'll do something about all those loose ends and also get rid of some of the pegs.

The photo opposite (bottom right) shows the simple way the ends are tied off. It doesn't *look* too secure, but don't worry — they will stay in place.

Step 2, half-finished. Continue filling until you reach the front.

Step 3 is just a repeat of step 1. No weaving yet!

leave the rest until you get to them.

Step 4: Now you start weaving. The top photo on page 76 shows the beginning of this step as it starts in the same hole as you used to begin Step 2. Study the photo carefully. You will weave *over the top* canes and *under the bottom* canes. It is especially important now that you keep the cane right-side up, because if it twists as you pull it through, you'll probably have to take it out again to straighten the strand.

An important material comes into use here: as you pull the strand through your fingers to ensure that the right side is up, have a little petroleum jelly on them so as to lubricate the cane. If you fail to do this, the friction of the canes sliding over each other as you pull the strand through the weave will melt, weaken, and even break, the strands already in place. The closer you get to completing the seat, the more necessary it becomes to properly lubricate the strands.

You will notice as you look at the bottom photo on page 76 that after you reach the left side and start back across, the weaving pattern looks identical to

This is how you tie off. This shows one knot completed and one being formed on the same loop.

Most of these knots will have other strands over them, and this helps to secure them. You can now tie off only the ends that have a loop next to them; those that don't are left until later. Neatness counts here. I have observed that the main difference between professional and amateur work in any field is usually *how the parts are finished that do not normally show.* The professional's finished work will be neat and well done, showing pride in his or her craft, while that of the amateur will often be sloppy and show lack of planning. Your first seat can look like that of a pro if you take a little care in tying off. Keep all the ends pointing in the same direction, and cut them all the same length. You can remove all the pegs where you managed to tie off;

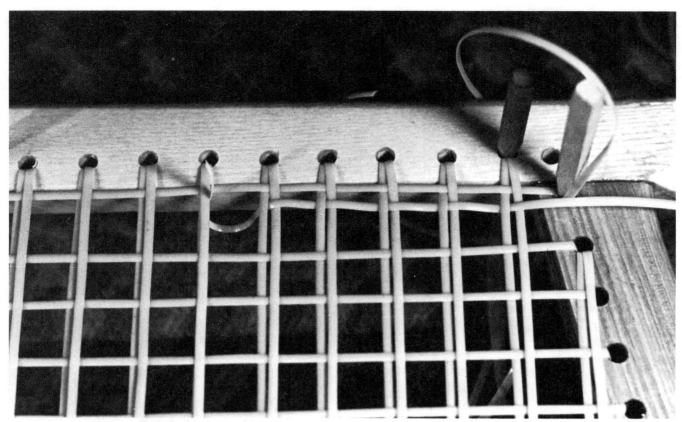

Step 4 is the first weaving step. "Over the top canes, under the bottom canes."

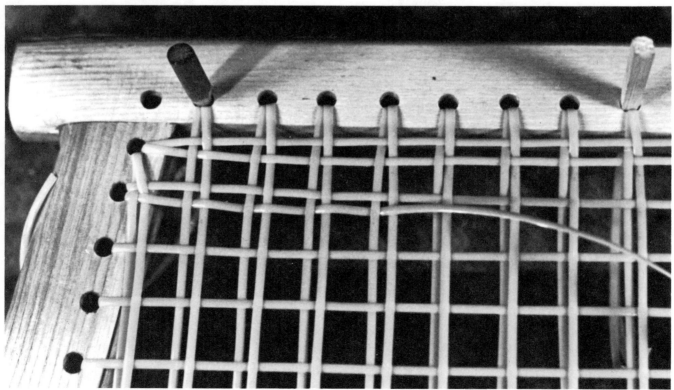

Step 4, continued. Going back across, you go over and under the same canes, but the order you do it must be reversed. Now it's "under the bottom canes, over the top canes."

Step 4, complete. At this point, push together and straighten out the woven pairs in preparation for the diagonal weaving.

that of the first strand. If you, like I do, keep yourself weaving correctly when going from right to left by repeating "over the top, under the bottom," then when you start going from left to right, reverse the phrase and say: "under the bottom, over the top." Same thing; different order. Be conscientious about keeping this under-and-over weave consistent; it will prevent confusion when you make the diagonal weaves in Steps 5 and 6.

Keep weaving back and forth across the seat until you reach the front and your seat looks like the above photo. By now, the weave should have tightened up a bit, and what you're working on is beginning to look and feel like a seat. Tie off each end as soon as there is a convenient loop to do so. In this and in future weaving steps, give the strand a little stretch after it is pulled in place across the seat. When you do this, you will feel the cane give a little, and it will stay in place, held tightly by the

weave of which it is now a part.

Step 5: Now the fun begins — making the diagonal cross-weaves that complete the pattern. The first diagonal starts in the right rear corner and weaves under the pairs of cane running from side to side and over the pairs running from front to rear. The top photo, page 78, shows the beginning of this step, and the bottom photo shows the step with a couple of strands in place and another one started. The pen in the bottom photo points to where the diagonal crosses the other weave. It slides in between the canes in the square weave, and runs straight and true. If it does not, you have probably reversed the sequence in Step 4, and things will not look right, even if you are now using the correct sequence. Don't despair; simply reverse the sequence in this step and in Step 6, and everything will look okay. Keeping the pattern straight will be simpler, if you have followed along with me.

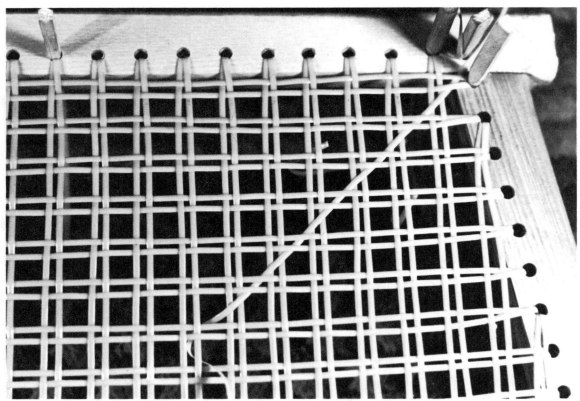

Step 5 is your first diagonal weave. You will go under the pairs running from left to right and over the pairs running from front to rear.

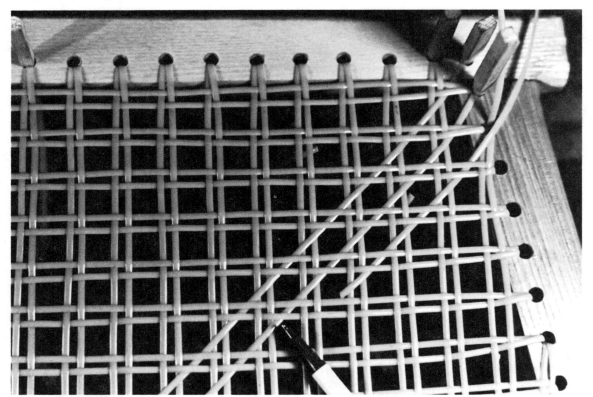

This begins the third pass of Step 5. The pen shows how the diagonal slides into the woven square, allowing it to run straight and true.

Step 5, about half done. Continue until you completely fill the seat.

Starting Step 6, the second diagonal weave. Now, you go over the pairs running from left to right and under the pairs running from front to rear.

Step 6, about half done. Now it's starting to look like something!

As you do your diagonal weaving, you will find that it is necessary to either skip a hole in the frame or to double up on one from time to time in order to keep the strands running parallel and evenly spaced with each other and looking neat. This is all right; it's to be expected because all four sides of your frame are not equal, yet each receives an equal number of canes. Take a look at the right side of the top photo on page 79, and you will see where I doubled up on one hole in two different places.

The photo on page 79 shows Step 5 completed on one side of the seat. From here, you simply fill in the other side as you did the first. Before you string that second corner strand, though, keep in mind that the corners will look better if you can space your strands to get two diagonal canes coming out of each corner hole. In the trade this is called a "Bird's Head," and it does look nice, though it is not essential. (See photo on page 82.) Don't forget that little tug after each strand is in place; it really tightens things up. Tie off as you go along or when it is convenient. Don't tie off the

canes in the corner holes. Leave the pegs there; we'll finish the corners a little later.

Step 6:   This step starts in the left rear corner and makes just the opposite diagonal weave of the sequence for Step 5. You will weave over the pairs running from side to side and under the pairs running from front to rear. The bottom photo on page 79 shows the beginning of this step, and the photo above shows it with one side completed. It is increasingly important that you keep those canes lubricated, because the weave is getting tighter and tighter as you go along. If you have to cut off a cane or two, it will be one of those you put in way back in Step 1 or 2. It isn't impossible to repair it, but it is a pain in the neck to have to.

About now you may have a little trouble getting the cane up and down through the holes. This is where the awl (a nail works well, too) comes in. Just push it down through the hole and push the cane aside to make room for the new strand.

The photo on page 82 shows that I managed to make the "Bird's Head" double diagonals in all

80

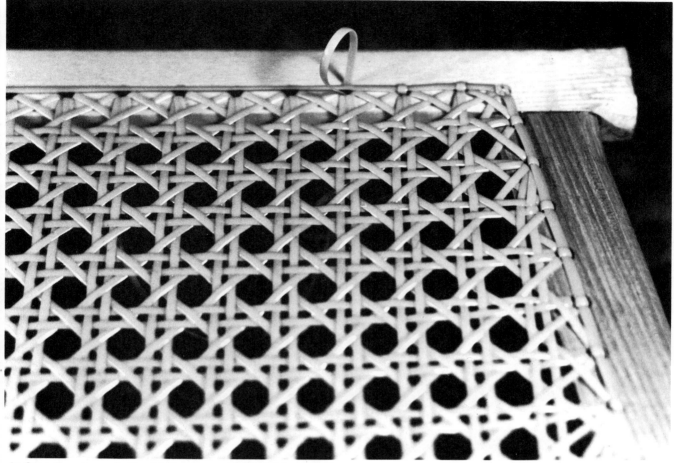

In Step 7, you apply the binder cane, the finishing touch.

corners but the right front one. I could have manipulated the spacing to do it there too, but didn't think it important enough to undo the work I'd done.

Step 7: This step is called the binder, and it is the finishing touch to your caning job. Remember that little bundle of cane that came with the regular cane? It is to be bound neatly around the edges, and is a little wider than the medium cane you are using so that it will cover up the holes. However, if you didn't get this wider cane, no problem. Use the regular cane; it is almost as good, and a lot better than no binder at all.

Start by cutting a length of binder cane that is 2″ or 3″ longer than the distance between the corner holes on the side you are starting first. Pull it tight, and peg each end into the corners. Now tie off a length of regular cane near the hole next to one of the corner holes, and come up through the hole. Keeping the cane right-side up, put it right back down through the same hole, making a loop over the binder cane. Come up through the next hole,

and repeat the process across the side until the other corner is reached. Peg in another length of binder from that corner to the next one, and continue securing the binder with the regular cane until you have gone all the way around the seat. The above photo shows how the binder should look when it is in place and also shows a loop ready to be pulled into place.

When you have completed the binding, you should have a peg at each corner. If your pegs are made of hardwood (as dowels), replace them with softwood (i.e., cedar) pegs. Drive the softwood pegs securely into the holes, score them with a knife even with the surface of the seat, and break them off. (I did this a little prematurely for the photo above so that it could be seen close-up.)

Congratulations — you did it! Your seat is finished. The photo on page 82 shows the seat I caned with everything in place, ready to be installed in a canoe. I know yours looks as good and probably better. Get the other one done, and launching will be right around the corner.

There we have it. One canoe seat — ready to install.

Alternative Seats

You say the ice is out, and you don't have time to spend on caning right now? Well, read on — there is a way to rig temporary seats, so that you can get out on the water.

If you have made the frames as described in this chapter, just buy some of the plastic webbing that is sold for use on lawn furniture. Stretch and weave it across your frame, and you will have some *fairly* comfortable seats for the season. The caning project can be delayed until next winter. Of course, almost any material that can be stretched across and secured to the frames will do.

If the seat frame construction has to be delayed too, you can always just hang a piece of plywood in the same manner as regular seats and rough it for the summer. Then you will really appreciate the caned seats next season.

The seat shown in the photo to the right is one that a student made in preference to a caned seat. The frame is simple. Two pieces of ¾" by 1½" hardwood stock were drilled to receive two pieces of 1" dowel. The dowels were glued and pegged in place. This student made use of his snowshoe-

building skills to produce the weave with 1/8" nylon cord, but there are any number of materials and weaves that could be used.

These are just some ideas that will put you on the water a little sooner. You may have others. Use your imagination and what you have on hand; but remember, your fine strip canoe deserves the best, so plan on caning those seats eventually. Besides, you will be able to use your caning skills to fix up any chairs that have been collecting dust in the attic.

Another way.

Installing the Seats

As mentioned before, the lengths shown in Figure 9 are purposely left long so they can be trimmed to fit when you install the seats. First, position your seats. The stern seat should be as far to the rear as you can get it, so you will probably trim off the horizontal pieces nearly right down to the frame itself. The front seat can vary according to individual taste and need (and leg length of the bow person), but a good starting point is about 40" to 45" from the stem. If you have made the tapered seats, install them so that the sides taper along with the sides of the canoe.

The seats are hung from the gunwales with ¼" carriage bolts (brass if you can get them). You will need two 6" bolts and six 4" ones. You will need an 18" length of 3/8" copper or steel tubing (larger will do as well); or instead you could drill out a dowel. The photo below shows seats hung with tubing spacers, and the photo above shows one hung with dowel spacers.

Line up the seats and drill holes down through the gunwales. Drill mounting holes in the seats so they will be well aligned with the holes in the gunwales. The holes in the gunwales may have to be at a slight angle to ensure that they will emerge inside the canoe and not continue into the hull. It is a good idea to make the holes a little oversize (use a 5/16" drill bit). With the canoe sitting level, use a level as you position the seats and measure for the correct length of the spacers. Cut them to length. The measuring is best accomplished by temporarily mounting the seat with the carriage bolts.

If you would like to have lower seats, they can be installed with longer bolts, but I have found that the 4" and 6" lengths work well. However, these lengths may vary from one canoe model to another.

Seat in place.

I like to have the heads of the carriage bolts holding the seats countersunk below the surface of the gunwales. If you want to do this, just find a spade bit or other type of bit that has the same or slightly larger diameter than that of the head of the carriage bolt, and drill about ¼" deep into the gunwale where the bolt is to be installed. This is best accomplished *before* the hole is drilled through the gunwale for the carriage bolt.

That's it. You're done! You may want to touch up with varnish where you have drilled to install the seats, but this is minor. As long as you have already varnished everything, the touch-up can come later. For now — head for the nearest water!

Seat hanger.

Summary of materials and tools needed to make the seats:

Materials

Hardwood stock, ¾" × 1½", 15' (linear)

Waterproof glue   Sandpaper

Fasteners, dowels or screws (see text)

Polyurethane varnish   Petroleum jelly

Medium cane, 1 roll or hank with binder

Carriage bolts — ¼"; two 6", and six 4", with nuts

Copper or steel tubing, 3/8", 18" long (or dowels; see text)

Tools

Table saw	¼" drill bit
Electric hand drill	Hammer
Sander	Knife
Rule	Awl or nail
Handsaw	Pegs for caning,
5/16" drill bit	18 or more

GUIDE: I compromised several designs, in this canoe, to meet my own needs. My canoe is usually loaded more heavily than those of my guests, so I like the extra length. I eliminated some of the rocker so that it would cut the water a little more smoothly and move more easily with a heavy load. The Guide loses a little maneuverability, but usually one advantage must give way to another.

Other Designs

I often wonder if it is really possible to come up with a truly "new" canoe design. The canoe is an ancient craft; it has existed for a couple thousand years, during which time variations could have been tried by tens of thousands of canoe designers. It is true that the evolution of modern canoes has been influenced by the evolution of modern canoe-building materials. Shapes are possible with today's plastics that would be impossible to attain with naturally occurring materials like wood and bark. A perusal through a manufacturer's catalog or through a canoeing magazine reveals dozens of far-out designs of canoes that I like to call (with tongue-in-cheek) "super-canoes." They are designed for maximum performance in the water, with little thought given to aesthetics.

How important are aesthetics, anyway? I think they are very important, having much to do with why we go canoeing in the first place. I think we go out on the water because there we can, for a short time at least, return to a different time and way of living. It's a return to nature, a link with the past. Most of us do *not* go canoeing to travel at the maximum speed possible with a people-powered craft. However, if maximum speed and efficiency are considered important, as by the canoe-racing fraternity, well then, the super-canoe is the craft.

I bring up aesthetics at this point because, if you are going to build a canoe for recreational use and want to design a little of yourself into it, you'll want a canoe that is pleasing for you to look at, to build, and to use. If this translates to you as a super-canoe, then go for it! If, like me, you're a bit of a romantic, you will stay closer to the more traditional designs. If you are a canoe-racing enthusiast, I don't have to tell you where to look for stations to build a strip racer; there have been many of them in every race I have attended, and the brotherhood of racers seem to be a cooperative bunch.

The phrase "I designed my own canoe" has a nice ring to it, but I'm not sure I can honestly say that I have designed from scratch. I guess it is a matter of interpretation. Designing can mean adapting an existing model to suit your needs, or sitting down with nothing more than a pencil, blank paper, and an idea to come up with a design that is, to the designer at least, original. My own experience is limited to the methods of adaptation and trial-and-error.

Back before I copied and made patterns from the two original E. M. White guide canoes, I needed a 20' guide canoe for my own use in my summer guiding business. Not having any suitable models to go by, I set out to design my own. It was successful, and I used it for several seasons until the Whites came along. Since I have had a life-long love affair with White-designed canoes, I adopted the 20' White Guide model as my personal canoe. Although my original Guide is a design I no longer build, its evolution still serves well to show how to go about adapting a base design. (The "Guide" referred to from here on is *my* Guide, not White's beautiful water creature.)

Making Your Own

The Guide's ancestry shows the adaptation process at work: the Guide evolved from the River Run-

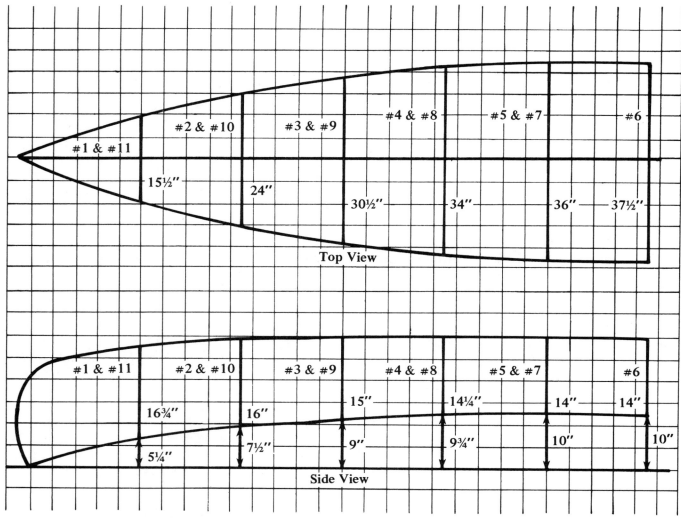

FIGURE 13 · Dimensions of Stations and General Shape of the 19' River Runner

ner, which had been modeled after a friend's canoe whose lines I particularly liked. So, you can see how a few changes here and there can create a new canoe.

The Guide, as I pictured it, was a combination of features that I had seen and admired. This canoe in my mind had a wide, flat bottom that would handle heavy loads. Its bow was not too wide, with not too much rocker, so as to cut the water without too much effort. Its stems were reasonably low so as not to catch the wind. I was willing to sacrifice a little whitewater maneuverability because I was building the canoe for my own use, and I knew I had the strength and experience to overcome any sluggishness in turning. (As it turned out, in practical use, this sluggishness I was willing to live with never raised it ugly head, and the Guide handled very well in whitewater.)

I chose the River Runner as a base model for my design, primarily because I liked the proportions of the cross section. Well pleased with the wide, flat bottom and tumblehome, I could concentrate on the ends. So, to shape the design to suit my needs I had to narrow the ends, reduce the rocker, change the sheerline, and increase the length by 1'. The latter was the easiest modification — I spaced the stations 20″ apart rather than 18″, and placed the stems 20″ apart rather than 24″. (This 20′–20″–20″ ratio is a coincidence in 20′ canoes; follow directions for spacing elsewhere in this book.)

Figure 13 was simple to make. I just plotted the dimensions of the stations on graph paper. Then I drew in the stations and the outline of the canoe along the edge of the stations — sort of like connecting the dots in a children's puzzle! The larger you make the sketches, the more accurate you can

86

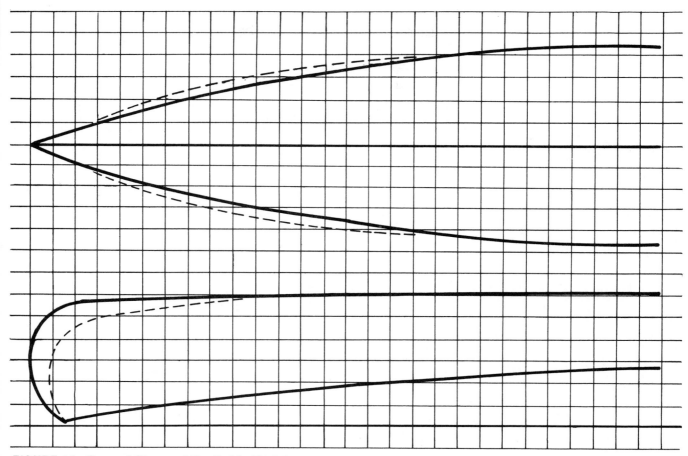

FIGURE 14 · General Shape of the Guide Model
This sketch was made by tracing Figure 13 (shown by broken lines), then making adaptations.

be in plotting the dimensions.

I made Figure 14 by placing a blank piece of graph paper over Figure 13 and drawing the new shape that I had in mind, thus using the River Runner lines as a guide. Once Figure 14 was as accurate as I could make it, I drew in the stations, making careful measurements to determine the Guide's proposed dimensions. This brought about Figure 15. To be sure, you will need to juggle and remeasure the figures before making patterns. You'll see the logic behind the adjustments as you develop your own sketches.

Now with the sketch of the new Guide in hand, I transferred it to pattern paper. For each station I marked the dimensions on the pattern paper — width, height, height of sheer, etc. Next, I took each corresponding station from the River Runner and, using it as a guide, drew the station for the canoe. In general, I followed the outline of each old station, but kept it within the limits of the new dimensions that I had marked previously on the pattern paper.

Once I had drawn all of the stations and stem patterns, it was time to cut the stations out of plywood and try the new design. Before doing this, however, I laid the station patterns one on top of the other, looked them over, and compared them to the River Runner patterns. Sometimes this will reveal problems that can be corrected in the pattern stage rather than the more difficult-to-correct plywood-station stage. Look for places where abrupt changes in dimension take place from one station to the next. If something doesn't look right, go back and recheck. This eyeballing isn't foolproof — sometimes what looks way out of whack turns out to be just right — but it *does* give you a chance to double-check. When the patterns were as accurate as I could make them, I got out the plywood.

I made the plywood stations and mounted them on the strongback with 20″ spacing. Next I laid trial strips along the sheerline and at 4″ intervals over the hull on one-fourth of the form so that I could visualize the lines of the new hull. Any

87

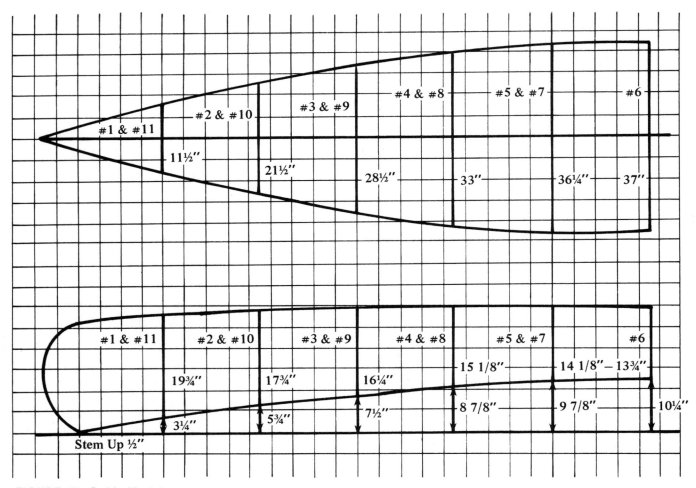

FIGURE 15 · Guide Model
The stations and dimensions have been filled in, working from the outline drawn in Figure 14.

awkwardness in the line can be corrected at this point by adding or sawing off wood from both sides of the offending station. Make sure that you alter the corresponding twin station on the other end of the canoe. To add wood to a station, just glue and nail a scrap of plywood along the edge in the problem area and re-saw to the corrected outline.

When satisfied with the line shown by the trial strips, I removed them and began to build the hull with permanent strips. Here and there, a small problem may arise during the final laying of strips that did not reveal itself with the trial strips, but corrections can almost always be made without removing strips. These minor corrections that are made during the stripping operation are the refinements that produce good, smooth hull patterns. Seldom are adaptations perfect the first time. When the perfectly smooth set of stations does emerge, make a permanent pattern from them for future use.

Most of the patterns in this book bear at least some small modification of my own— except for the Whites, which are as close to the original as I could make them. Of these models, probably the Wabnaki is the closest to being my own design. It evolved through experience in building and using canoes, and the result is one that I have been proud of, and have taken satisfaction in seeing people build and use.

There is a great deal of satisfaction in designing and building a canoe yourself. If you think you have the "feel" of canoe design, give it a try. The systematic approach described and illustrated here can be followed for minor or major modifications. You can study, consider, and doodle on the preliminary sketches before proceeding to cut up expensive material. When you are done, you can scrap the patterns or you can proceed with the project; and who knows, maybe you'll come up with the perfect canoe.

Copying the Old (or New) Masters

Copying an admired canoe isn't the ordeal it might seem. All you need is a couple of reference lines from which to measure and a systematic approach to the problem. Think of the stations as "slices" from the cross section of the canoe which are set at certain distances above the strongback. All you need to do is determine the exact shape of the slices and how far above the strongback each one is positioned. The following photographs show how to do this.

It helps to have an extra pair of hands to help hold things in place while you are scribing those lines, but you can do it alone if you are careful. Think about each step! You have to turn the copied canoe upside down in your mind to see how the patterns should be made. Once you fully understand the method and purpose of each step, you will have no trouble.

Trial strips.

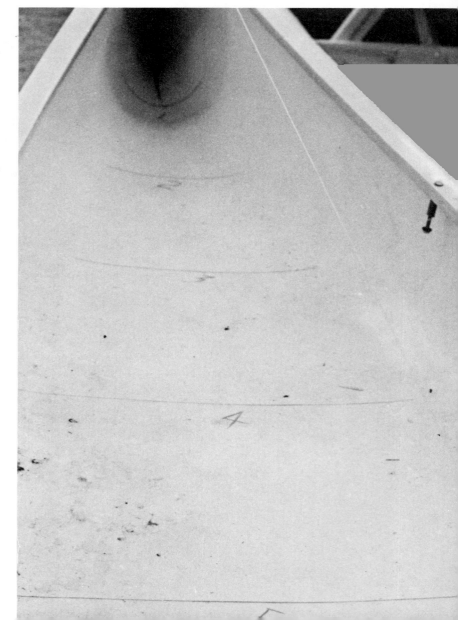

(Above) The first step is to stretch a line taut between the stem points. This line represents the top of the strongback for the canoe that you are going to build, and gives a common reference line from which to take measurements.

(Right) Now, starting at the center, draw parallel lines on the bottom of the canoe every 18", or whatever spacing you decide is appropriate. The lines indicate the placement of the stations for the canoe you are going to build. They should be perpendicular to the centerline of the canoe. You can number these lines for reference, if you wish. Only half the canoe needs to be marked — the other end is identical.

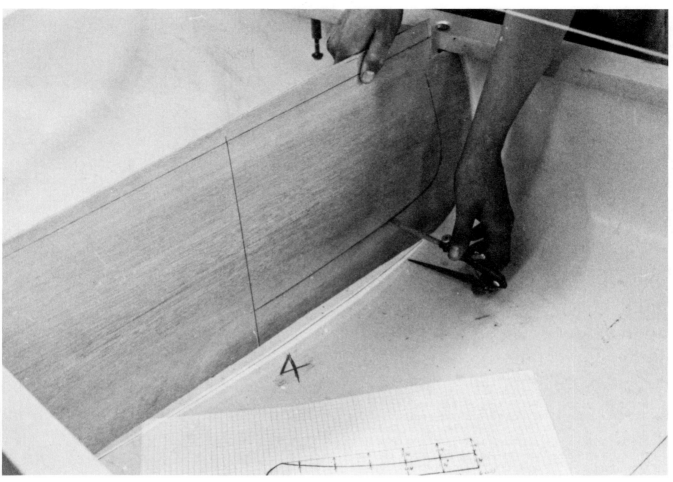

(Above) Next, cut a piece of cardboard, old paneling, or whatever you have on hand, so that it will roughly fit into the canoe. Set your compass for a radius of 2", then scribe each line halfway around the cross section of the canoe. The compass setting is actually not important; just maintain the same setting *throughout the scribing process*. Take care to keep the compass legs perpendicular to the panel.

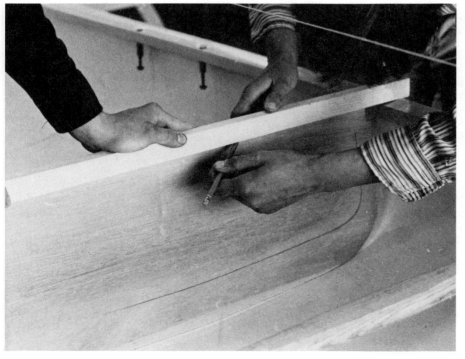

(Left) Before you move the panel that you have scribed onto, lay a straightedge across the gunwales and draw a line across the top of the panel to establish the gunwale line. Also, measure from gunwale to gunwale so as to determine the exact center of the canoe at each point. This centerpoint is essential because you are using half patterns.

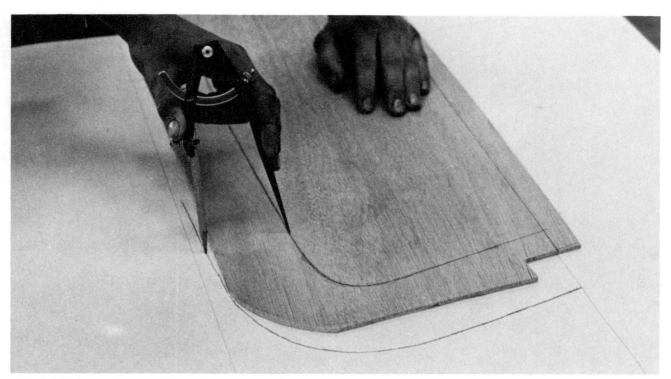

(Above) Remove the panel from the canoe and place it on your pattern sheet. Leaving your compass at the same setting as before, follow the line on the panel with one leg of the compass while the other leg marks the pattern sheet. The line on the pattern will be an exact tracing of the canoe. Now, all you need are the measurements from the strongback to the bottom of the canoe.

(Right) To measure from the strongback to the canoe bottom, read the intersection of the perpendicular rule with the strongback line (align the rule with the midpoint of the gunwale line). Raise the rule and measure from the straightedge placed from gunwale to gunwale to the strongback line to determine the strongback-to-gunwale distance. (Note the graph paper sketch in the bottom of the canoe. This is on hand to record measurements as they are taken, and to jot down notes.)

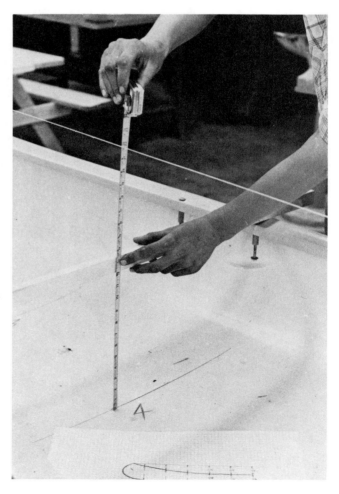

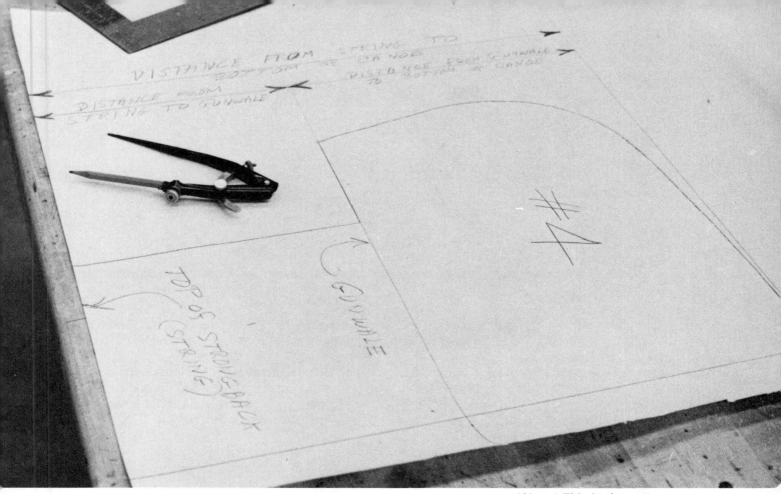

DISTANCE FROM STRING TO
BOTTOM OF CANOE

DISTANCE FROM
STRING TO GUNWALE

DISTANCE FROM GUNWALE
TO BOTTOM OF CANOE

GUNWALE

#4

TOP OF STRONGBACK
(STRING)

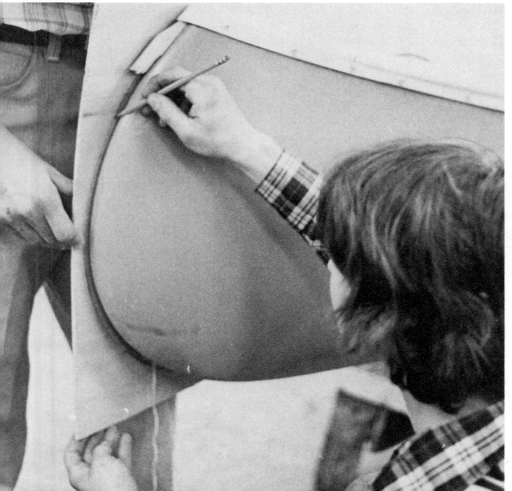

(Above) This is the pattern sheet, complete with the scribed form and all recorded measurements. The bottom of the paper marks the strongback or stem-to-stem line; the step where the scribed portion begins represents the gunwale line. The other measurement is from the strongback line to the bottom of the canoe. This completes the pattern for one station; repeat the same procedure for each of the others.

(Left) The only remaining task is to make a tracing of the stem. The photo is self-explanatory — but do remember to trace the stem-to-stem line onto the panel. The stem form pattern is cut on this line. It is the part of the stem form that sits on the strongback.

Repairs

Sooner or later you have to take your pride and joy out onto the water. That beautifully crafted strip canoe is, after all, not made to be on exhibit forever for you and your friends to admire. Face up to it, and when you hear that first scratch grinding into your lovingly polished finish, amplified in your mind way beyond the actual damage being done, just tell yourself that this is what you made it for — to use! Also remember, you can be comfortable in the knowledge that you know how to build a canoe, so even if the worst happens (heaven forbid), you can still go back to your strongback and put together a new canoe, better than the first, with your new-found skills.

Fiberglassed strip canoes are tough, but they have their limits, and if you use yours extensively you will eventually learn what those limits are. I put 500 to 700 miles of water travel per year on my own 20′ White Guide model — about half of it on rivers, and by the end of the season, very shallow rivers! In 15 years of rigorous use, by myself and by my guests on river trips, I have had to develop the fine art of making repairs.

My switch to epoxy resin has greatly decreased the extent of patching and repairs that I have had to make, and this is why I am such a devoted convert. As I see it, there are three major factors that make the epoxy resin preferable over polyester. The first is that the resin penetrates the wood and seals it so well that when there *is* a break in the fiberglass, water does not enter the wood to cause delamination problems. The second is that the resin is such a good adhesive that the fiberglass layers are, as far as I can see, impossible to separate from the wood. The third factor is that the resin is flexible and so allows the canoe to "give" with impact, which helps prevent damage in many cases.

I have found that a canoe is most subject to damage when it is out of its element. As I write this, my 20-footer lies on its rack waiting for repairs. The damage was done not on the water this past summer in the canoe's 700 miles of travel, but on dry land. I use it occasionally during the November hunting season, and so I left it on my lawn, handy for the next time I might want to use it. While I was away from home on a hunting trip, we had some extremely high winds. My family didn't think soon enough to secure the canoe, and it went tumbling down the hill, with the result that one gunwale was shattered near the bow, a hole was bashed in the side where the canoe must have landed with its full weight on a rock or fencepost, and one of the thwarts was broken. All of this damage would be almost impossible to accomplish on the water.

Another common cause of damage to canoes is improper securing for transportation on a car rack. This only happened to me once. (I may be careless, but I'm not stupid!) A gust of wind hit the side of my car, and the next thing I knew, I was looking in the rear-view mirror watching a *brand-new* strip canoe tumble end over end down the road behind me. When I assessed the damage, I found one broken gunwale strip and multiple abrasions, and two thwarts and one seat had popped out. Except for drying time, I spent a total of two hours in the shop making the necessary repairs. This says something for my method of handling stem reinforcement, because the canoe tumbled stem over stem on the pavement. I only had to patch up the abrasions where the pavement quickly rasped off the fiberglass.

What happens when you or your partner makes a mistake, and — "CRUNCH" — a hole? One of

Cutting out a delaminated section of fiberglass. A small burr was used in the tool shown here, but a wood chisel works just as well.

the great things about the multi-layer construction of a strip canoe is that a hole is almost always not a hole in the usual sense of the word — that is, the water does not come gushing in as it would in some other forms of construction. What happens is that there is a break in the *outside* layer of fiberglass. This break will eventually allow water to enter the wood layer of the fiberglass-wood-fiberglass sandwich, but this takes time. As soon as you discover the break, a strip of duct tape will be all of the patching that is needed for the duration of your trip, be it one day or three weeks. Duct tape or a similar plastic patching tape is all the repair material I take on my wilderness canoe trips.

The more heavily loaded the canoe and the harder it hits that offensive rock, the more damage it is possible to do. The broken wood shown in the photo on page 97 is about the extreme of damage that I have done on the water, short of a complete wipeout by broaching on a rock in heavy rapids. Even with the canoe in the photos, where all three

layers were broken, there was no rapid entrance of water. The wood fibers come back together and make an effective seal so that the water only seeps in, which gives ample time to get ashore and make necessary temporary repairs.

It is the small break in the outside layer of fiberglass, unnoticed among the many scratches, that causes the most extensive damage, especially on canoes built with polyester resin. Here, the water seeps in and does its work of separating the outside layer of fiberglass from the wood, completely unnoticed until the area is large like that shown in the photos. This delaminated area is first noticed as a whitish spot (sometimes it gets to 8″ or 10″ in diameter if you are not paying attention), and when you push it, you can see the water trapped between the layers.

The photos in this chapter, showing a repair to a polyester-fiberglassed canoe, illustrate probably the most difficult repair job you'd be faced with. If you used epoxy resin on your canoe, the size of

Removing the fiberglass.

your patch will be miniscule compared with this one. The epoxy will hardly delaminate at all due to the tenacious bond it makes with the cedar. Thus, if you *do* have to repair, it will be a very small patch. The repair procedure that follows, therefore, is for the polyester job. For repair of an epoxy-glassed canoe, the steps are the same, except that you will not have nearly as large an area to worry about.

Usually you cannot be sure how much delamination exists until you start removing the fiberglass; so start small, right around the break, and work outward until you reach the point where the fiberglass adheres to the wood. Don't overdo this; it is possible to continue pulling away the fiberglass, even from the "healthy" areas (not as likely with epoxy). The small grinding tool shown in the photo on page 95 does a nice job of cutting through the fiberglass, but a wood chisel works just as well, and it will start the feathering process by cutting the old fibergasss at an angle.

Once the fiberglass is removed, the wood must be allowed to thoroughly dry out. You can hasten this process with heat lamps or some other heat source. Just be sure the wood is dry before you continue with the repair. If the fiberglass layer on the inside of the canoe is also broken, you will have to repair that, too. Usually you needn't remove that fiberglass because the wood can dry through the outside, but if there is delamination there too, you'll have to remove it. Generally, sanding around the inside rip and applying a patch of fiberglass will take care of it. However, do this later while fiberglassing the outside.

When the wood is dry, proceed as follows: with the power sander, thoroughly sand the exposed wood and the fiberglass 3″ or so beyond the open area. Feather the edges of the old fiberglass. If any of the cedar strips were cracked and dislodged, try to fit them back into place. Once dry, they usually pop back where they belong with a little gentle prying and tapping. When everything has been sanded, mix up a little resin and seal the wood with it, as you did when building the canoe — way back when.

Sanding and feathering the edges.

Let the sealer cure for the recommended time.

When the sealer is ready to be worked, give it a light sanding and then bring out those scraps of cloth that you saved during construction. Cut out two patches the exact size and shape of your opening, and lay them on; this should more or less even up the surface. Cut out another patch, enough larger than the first ones to overlap the good fiberglass of your canoe by 1″ to 1½″. (This outer patch will thus be 2″ to 3″ larger in diameter than the opening.)

Mix up your resin, and soak the patches just as in construction. Start by soaking the two patches that fit inside the opening; then lay on the overlapping patch. All are wetted out at the same time — that is, with one mix of resin. You will have only one edge (that of the largest patch) to sand and feather out for the final finish. If you feel it is practical at this time, you can lay a patch on the inside while you still have active resin. Otherwise, do it later with another patch.

Every repair is different — you just have to use good judgment and common sense. Sometimes more extensive repairs than I have described are required on the inside, but not often.

Once the patches have cured, sand them well, paying particular attention to the edge of that last and largest patch. Feather it down. Now mix up a little more resin and give the area another coat, and continue the sanding and filling until the weave of the fabric is filled. *Don't yield to the temptation to give the entire hull another coat of resin.* Many people cannot resist, as the resin appears to rejuvenate the finish. Beyond the immediate good looks, though, it does nothing but add weight and cause trouble down the road. And remember, you have a couple of coats of varnish on that hull! Resin will not adhere to it well, and peeling will result in a short time. If you want to refinish, do it by sanding the entire hull and giving it another coat or two of varnish.

Your repair is finished. If you decided to sand

Fiberglass patch cut to fit.

and refinish the canoe, the damaged area will be hard to find; otherwise, you will have to wait until the scratches of daily use make the shiny new patch blend with the rest of the hull. Either way, you have a repair that is permanent and will not require your attention again. It is thicker than the rest of the hull now, and so if you have future problems with that partner of yours going the wrong way, the damage will be most likely to occur in an adjacent area, but not on the repair.

Repair jobs can sometimes betray you by developing small waves and bumps, depending on how careful you were in your feathering and finishing operation. However, don't worry about that too much. Like the scratches, these patches often bring back memories. Years later you will be pointing at them and proudly telling the story of how you got that hole running some canoe-eating river at flood stage.

I really enjoy the incredulous looks and comments I get from some people when they see me taking a wooden canoe through rapids. Seasoned whitewater canoeists know it can be done, of course, but to these novices it is just unbelievable that anyone would do such a thing.

If you do decide to do a lot of hard whitewater-running with your strip canoe, you might decide that you are going through this business of patching just a little too often for your taste. If you don't mind a little extra weight, consider putting another layer of fiberglass on the bottom. Cut the fabric to the football shape just as is described in the chapter on fiberglassing. Prepare your canoe by *completely* sanding off the varnish in the area to be covered — or the whole outside hull, if you want to refinish, too. Then just wet out the cloth and go through the same finishing operations as for the original work. If you are careful in feathering out the edge of the football, the layer will be impossible to detect when you are finished.

Are you still dissatisfied with that patched and scratched canoe? Well, what do you have planned this coming winter? Why not keep that strongback active, and make another canoe? I don't see how anyone can get along with just one, anyway.

Summary of materials and tools needed to make repairs:

Materials
Fiberglass fabric (three layers per patch)
Small amount of resin and hardener
2 or 3 sheets of 50- or 80-grit sandpaper

Tools:
Scissors
Wood chisel or other tool for cutting away damaged fiberglass
Power sander (not essential, but it helps)
Brushes or other tools for wetting out and applying finish coats of resin
Containers for resin
Goggles
Protective gloves and/or cream

Paddles

I have been trying to make decent paddles for almost as long as I have been building canoes, aiming for the following ideals: the paddles had to be strong, relatively lightweight, inexpensive and uncomplicated to build, and long lasting. I tried many, many experiments through the years, but it was not until I started using epoxy resin that I came up with a paddle I'm pleased with. One reason these paddles are inexpensive is that they are built almost entirely of materials that you will probably have left over from building your strip canoe — cedar, ash, fiberglass, and epoxy resin. The only additional material you will need is thickener for the epoxy to make glue.

If you've sneaked a look at Figure 16, you probably have figured out from the plans that the paddle is to have a rather wide blade and a finished length of 63″. Realize that these are the plans for my own paddle, and are intended for you to alter to suit your own needs.

How do you determine what you need for a paddle? Perhaps my own rationale will help you. When I paddle, my stroke is rather long and slow; I take somewhere between 22 and 25 strokes per minute. Thus, the wide paddle suits me. I am 6′1″ tall, and the usual criteria for paddle length is that it come to the nose when standing. This would suggest a 66″ paddle for me, but I have found that too long for my liking, and so I have shortened it to 63″. (In talking with others who do a lot of whitewater canoeing, I find that they also prefer a shorter paddle than the standard nose-length.)

Everyone who takes wilderness canoe trips should carry a spare paddle. My spare is 72″ long — a full 6′! The reason for this extra length is that in shallow water I often stand and paddle from that position in order to seek out the best channel, and

the six-footer is far more comfortable to use while standing. In the unlikely event that I should break my shorter paddle, I can get by with the longer one.

Design your paddle for the way you will use it. If you, like the fur-trading voyageurs, paddle at 60 strokes per minute, you certainly don't want a paddle blade that is 8″ or 9″ wide — you'll last about 15 minutes. (Theirs, by the way, were 3½″ to 4″ wide.) If you are 5′ tall, you don't want a 6′ paddle, even for paddling from an upright position. If you are starting out with little paddling experience to draw upon, use this as a starting point for your first paddle: have the length be somewhere between your chin and nose (mine comes to my chin), and the width between 6″ and 8″. Now, let's get started.

Take a look at the paddle parts shown on page 102. Two paddles are shown: one has four parts, the other three. (Neither one has an advantage over the other; the point is that there is more than one way to "paddle a canoe.") One necessary tool that you probably don't have is a surface planer, which is used to bring the various parts of the paddle to the proper thickness. If you don't have a local woodworking shop that can do it for you, try the high-school or vocational-shop teacher. (We're a congenial group.) The blade and the shaft core are of cedar and are ¼″ thick; these can be made as one or separately, as shown in the photo. The two shaft spines are of ash and are 5/16″ thick.

Although the two paddles shown here were made of solid pieces of wood, why not, if you have just made a strip canoe, make matching paddles? Take those leftover strips and glue them together on a scrap piece of plywood covered with plastic for easy release. When the glue has set, scrape and sand them, and you already have the blade and

A pair of strong, lightweight, flexible paddles.

Component parts for two paddles. Three- and four-part versions are shown.

shaft core that are the correct thickness, the makings of a strip paddle to go with your strip canoe. The same white glue you used for your canoe will do also for gluing the paddle strips, because, like your canoe, you will encase the paddle in epoxy.

When you have planed (or glued together) your material to the proper thickness and have modified the pattern to suit yourself, cut out the pieces, and get ready to glue them together. Here's where you'll need that thickener for the epoxy. The Gougeon Brothers recommend Microfibers as a thickener for the purpose of gluing, and I concur with their recommendation — it does a great job. But first, before mixing the adhesive, put the pieces of the paddle together, lining them up carefully, and drill three holes to receive alignment pins. Two pins will go near each end of the shaft through the two shaft spines and the core, and the third will go through the two spines and the upper portion of the paddle blade. (Of course, if your blade and shaft core are the one-piece version, only two pins will be needed for alignment.) The size of the holes

will depend on what size pins you use. The purpose of these pins is to help prevent the wood pieces from sliding out of alignment when you are clamping them up. They are to be a permanent part of the paddle. I use brass sometimes, and sometimes wooden dowels.

One last thing before you mix the epoxy: make a centerline on both sides of the paddle blade (the long way). This will enable you to accurately center the points of the shaft spines when you clamp the parts together. Also, you should now read ahead a few paragraphs, because you may want to further shape the ends of the spines before you apply that irrevocable glue.

When you are ready to put the paddle together, mix up the epoxy and thickener and spread the mixture on the parts to be joined. It is always a good practice when gluing to completely cover *both* surfaces to be joined. This helps eliminate any voids, or bare areas. One of the great things about this adhesive, besides the fact that it will not let go and is wonderfully flexible, is that it fills the slightest cavity and doesn't leave voids.

Now put the pieces together, align them with the pins, and clamp them up. I like to put the clamps every 6″ or so, but if you have a shortage of clamps, fewer will do — especially if you use a

Use enough clamps to ensure that there are no voids.

piece of angle iron or stiff hardwood to spread the pressure of the clamp over a larger area. With the thickened epoxy mixture it is not necessary (in fact, not recommended) to clamp the pieces too tightly. Don't squeeze *all* the glue from between the pieces to be joined. Check to ensure that everything is still lined up, because there can still be some sliding, even with the holding pins. When everything is to your satisfaction, set the assembly aside to harden for about 12 hours.

When the epoxy has hardened and the clamps are removed, it is time for the craftsman in you to step aside and let the artist take over. You will sculpt and shape the paddle until it is a beautiful and useful tool that will not only serve you for years of canoeing, but will give you a sense of accomplishment and pride whenever you hold it.

The first thing you have to do is trim down the shaft; it is too wide, to allow for some slippage. Make a centerline the length of the shaft, then measure ½″ each side of it and make lines parallel to the centerline. When you cut on these lines, the shaft will be 1″ wide and will have an even surface from which to start the shaping operation. Where

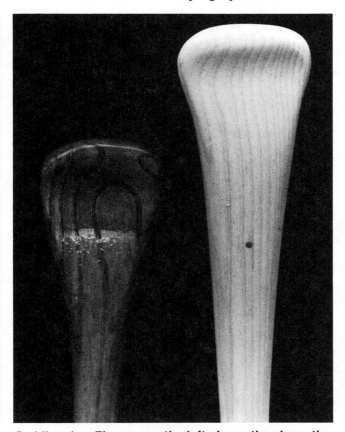

Paddle grips. The one on the left shows the sheen the bare wood takes on after a 500 – 600 mile season. (How many strokes?)

the shaft widens at each end you can widen your trim line accordingly to make a graceful flare at the grip and at the junction with the blade.

The hardest shaping job is that spear-shaped point on the end of each shaft spine where it overlaps the blade. The spines have to be tapered from nearly full thickness where the blade joins the shaft core to zero thickness at the very point; then the sides have to be feathered to smoothly join the blade. I have had good success in shaping this spear-shaped point *before* the parts are glued up. It requires careful work, because the wood is taken down to a knife edge where it is to meet the paddle blade. However, probably no more care is needed here than in dressing it down after the parts are together, because then you must take care not to cut into the soft cedar of the paddle blade.

Round off the shaft and shape the grip to what you feel is just right. The photo to the lower left shows the shape I give mine. The darker grip (left) is that of a paddle that I have used through an entire season. Note the lustre that the bare wood takes on after being worked in the palm of the hand for thousands of strokes.

When the rough shaping is done, continue the job with various grits of sandpaper until you have made the paddle smooth and free of tool marks. The blade, being only ¼″ thick, will not require much shaping. I taper the edge to about 1/8″. (We'll talk more about that edge when we get to the fiberglassing later on.) That cedar is soft, so be careful not to overdo the sanding and get it too thin.

When I am working in my shop on a project such as these paddles, I am the thorough craftsman; I bring the finishes to a much finer point than bare utility would demand. However, when I am out on the river with a party of canoeists, I make harsh demands upon my equipment, and I expect it to stand up, or I will use something else. One thing that happens is that in shallow water, to avoid hanging up, I often jab the end of the paddle into the rocky bottom to give the canoe a lift and the thrust to get by. Now, no one knows better than I that this is not a good way to treat a paddle blade, and I *do* always carry a pole, but the paddle is in my hands at the instant I need it, and right or wrong, I use it. Even if you are careful of the paddle tip, it is subject to damage from inadvertently struck rocks in shallow water. Here's how I protect my paddle blades:

Look closely at the blade tip in the photo on page 106. It is edged with a piece of 1/8″ nylon rope. That rope, thoroughly soaked with epoxy

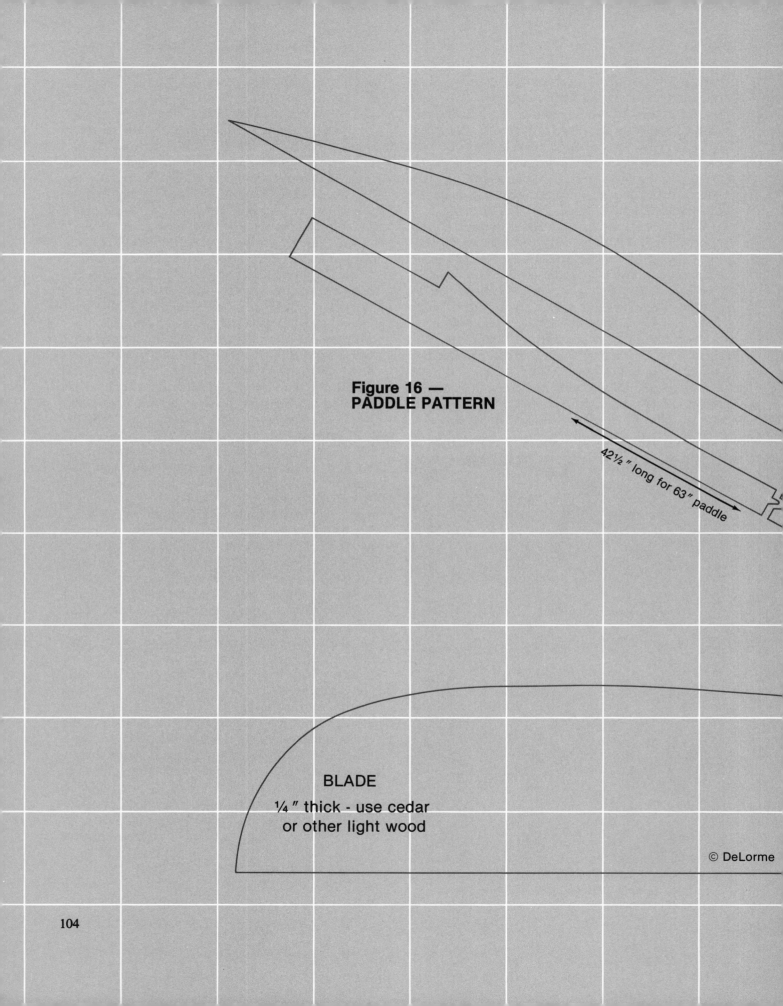

Figure 16 —
PADDLE PATTERN

42½″ long for 63″ paddle

BLADE

¼″ thick - use cedar
or other light wood

© DeLorme

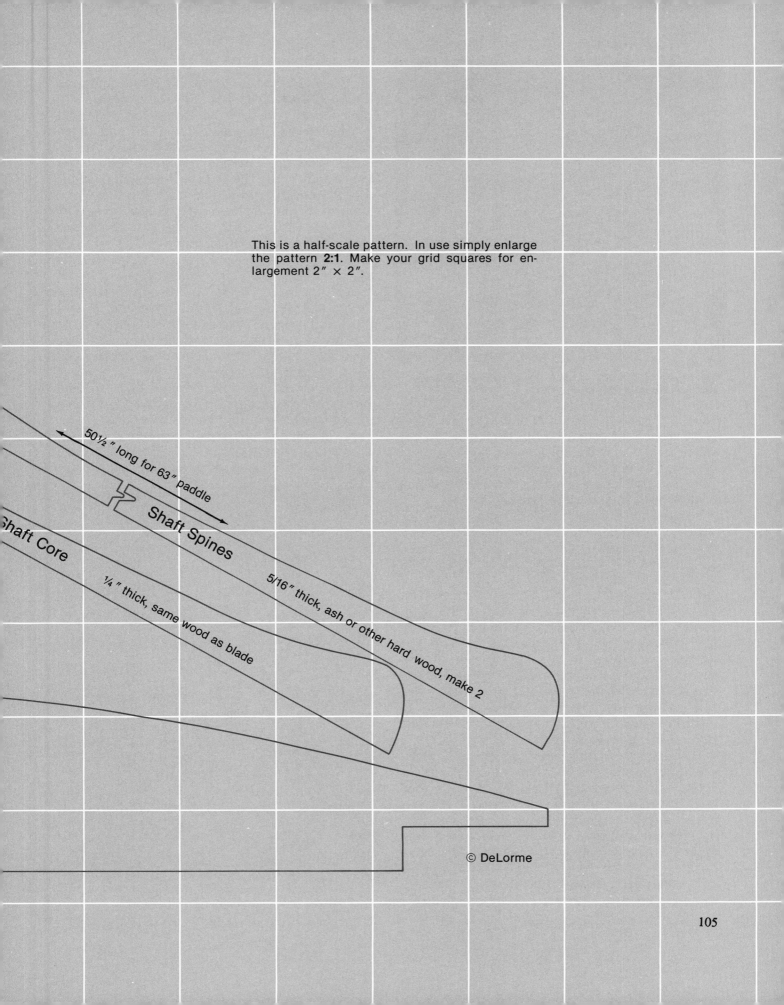

This is a half-scale pattern. In use simply enlarge the pattern **2:1**. Make your grid squares for enlargement 2″ × 2″.

50½″ long for 63″ paddle

Shaft Spines

Shaft Core

5/16″ thick, ash or other hard wood, make 2

¼″ thick, same wood as blade

© DeLorme

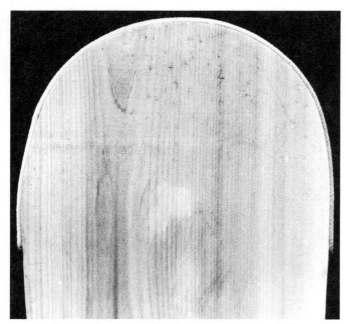

The reinforcing piece of nylon rope. Be sure it is well saturated with epoxy resin.

resin, was applied at the same time as the blade was given its sealer coat of epoxy in preparation for fiberglassing. That little piece of rope will give an amazing amount of protection once a layer of fiberglass cloth on each side of the blade has been brought to it and sealed in place with epoxy resin. When the sealer/rope epoxy has cured, give the surface a light sanding, and the blade is ready for a layer of fiberglass.

Only the blade of the paddle will be fiberglassed, up to the point where the blade meets the shaft core. Do one surface at a time to save yourself a lot of hassle. The fiberglass is applied in the usual manner, but pay particular attention to the edges of the blade, especially near the rope at the tip. Use an excessive amount of resin in these areas to ensure that the edges are thoroughly sealed and, particularly, that there is a good bond where the fiberglass lies over the rope. The excess resin will naturally gather at the edge anyway, but take time to be sure everything is covered.

If you want to permanently identify your paddle, this is the time to do it. Anything you put under the epoxied fiberglass will be hard to remove. I used my logo and name from my letterhead. I was surprised to find that the epoxy resin, when it soaked into the paper, caused it to nearly disappear, and made the logo and name stand out as if it were a decal.

You may have enough fiberglassing experience by now to know this already, but in case you don't,

I'll tell you, anyway: do not try to bring the fiberglass around the edge of the paddle and onto the opposite side. It just will not make a sharp enough fold to remain flat against the wood, but will bubble up, and you will end up sanding off most of it to make the edge smooth again. Just let the cloth lie flat naturally, as shown in the lower right-hand photo. The extra resin you put on at the edge will weight it some and cause it to bend partially over your tapered edge. When both sides have been fiberglassed, the edge will be covered with a fairly thick coat of epoxy.

When the first side has hardened, rough-trim the edge with a sharp knife, sand off any drips of epoxy that may have run around from the first side, and then fiberglass the other side. Again, watch your edges: the epoxy will really settle there now because you have the partially cured fiberglass edge from the first side to help hold it in place. Set aside, wet side up, to cure.

Once you have the fiberglass on, you can sand and apply as many coats of epoxy as you need to bring the blade to a smoothness that satisfies you. This will probably not be very many coats, because when you cover a flat, level surface, like the paddle blade, the epoxy can be flowed on, and a very

Wetting out the fiberglass. The squeegees work just as well for this, but we already had the roller out for another job.

If you used good wood, the paddle will not let you down.

glossy surface results. (Besides, you will be varnishing the paddle.) You will need to feather out the fiberglass edge at the top where the blade meets the shaft. Carefully done, the edge of the fiberglass will be invisible. Smooth up the edges of the blade with a fine rasp and sandpaper, and you should be ready to finish the shaft.

The shaft *and* the blade should be given the protection of the marine varnish that you used for the canoe. I like to give three coats. Do you varnish the grip or not? The old-timers say no, a varnished grip causes blisters. I have seen a lot of paddles with varnished grips, but have not seen any blisters on the grip hand. Lots of people get them on the other hand, but not on the grip hand. Tradition dies hard, and I have always preferred an unfinished grip. However, with a laminated paddle we have a problem: in spite of the super holding power of the epoxy glue, the forces of nature are stronger. The unprotected wood will absorb moisture over a period of time, and the force of the expanding wood will cause a slight delamination at the grip. Therefore, I have found it necessary to protect the grips with varnish. In fact, some resin applied on the shaft and grip before the varnish will afford even more moisture protection for the wood.

Another thing the old-timers put great store in was the flexibility of the paddle. A paddle was "no good" unless it had a "lot of flex." It was said that the shock transmitted to the shoulders from a too-stiff paddle caused fatigue — and, I suppose, all manner of other problems. Here again, there is room to doubt the necessity for flexibility. After all, it isn't as if you are jabbing the blade into the hard-packed ground all day; it's water we're pushing and pulling. But I took the photo here to show that our paddles have flexibility *and* strength as well.

I don't, as a rule, go around weighing paddles. I pick them up and heft them. If they feel right, then they *are* right. However, I happened to have in my shop a solid ash paddle, made by a well-known manufacturer and of the same dimensions as mine, so I couldn't resist weighing them both. The solid ash weighed in at 2 pounds, 11 ounces; mine was 1 pound, 14 ounces. Thirteen ounces lighter! Of course, this is only one comparison of many that could be made, but compared with most paddles I have handled, this one is light. Modesty almost prevents me from saying this, but what the hell: compared with other paddles I have handled, this one is the best.

Summary of materials and tools needed to make one paddle:

Materials

2 pieces of ash, 5/16″ × 4″ × 51″
1 piece of cedar, ¼″ × 4″ × 43″
1 piece of cedar, ¼″ × 9″ × 24″
   (Note: can replace cedar with strips, see text)
1 pound of epoxy resin
½ yard 6-ounce fiberglass cloth
½ ounce colloidal silica
3 alignment pins, 1″, brass, wood, or other
3 grits of sandpaper (see text)
2 coarse sanding discs for drill
1 pair of disposable gloves
30″ length of 1/8″ nylon rope
3 roller covers
½ pint varnish

Tools

Pencil	Bandsaw or sabersaw
Electric drill	1 roller frame
Drill bit, size for	1 tray for resin
alignment pins	1 sharp knife
6 C-clamps	Varnish brush
Wood rasp	Surface planer
Disc sander for drill	

Update for the Nineties ━━━━━━━━━━

In order to keep this book current and up-to-date I have asked the folks at DeLorme to allow me to use these pages to tell about new materials as well as the new little tricks and techniques that we have learned since this edition was first published. My thanks go out to the many people who have taken the time to write and pass on their hints and suggestions. The most satisfying thing about having written a book like this is hearing from the folks who have successfully used it.

Drywall Screws: Drywall screws, for the woodworker, are like paper towels and plastic bags to the camper. How, we ask ourselves, did we ever get along without them?

In the text you'll see nails recommended for those stubborn strips that staples can't quite hold down. It was a matter of months after this book went to press that I discovered how well drywall screws work to hold those stubborn strips in place. Now we use nothing else. The screws not only hold the strips more securely, but they have the added advantage of not doing as much damage to the plywood stations as do the nails.

Sealing and Filling: After the canoe is sanded it is always necessary to seal the wood before starting the fiberglassing. It is *usually* necessary to fill some holes and depressions where the stripping process didn't quite go as planned. I think it is always a good idea to fill the screw holes, if nothing else.

For a filling material I now use Gougeon's number 410 Microlight™ mixed with their epoxy resin to make a mixture that is about the consistency of putty. I have found that some 406 Colloidal Silica mixed in to the resin before adding the Microlight helps to get a more workable mix. This material is a light tan color and blends well with cedar, colorwise. We use the Microlight mix to fill the *larger* holes and allow it to cure before we do the final sanding. Then we proceed with the sealing and more filling as described in the following paragraph.

When the hull is ready for sealing roll the pre-pared epoxy material as described in the fiberglassing chapter. Next, mix up some Microlight putty and fill everything that seems to need it including the screw holes, cracks, depressions, or whatever. This putty is troweled over and into the holes with the squeegee while the sealer epoxy is still wet and no attempt is made to remove the excess putty during its application. When everything is filled, and you have an awful looking mess all over your canoe, take squeegees and remove everything from the surface, taking care to leave the canoe surface as smooth and free of filler as possible. Start at the center (keel line) of the canoe and squeegee down to the gunwale; then wipe *all* of the material from the squeegee before making the next pass.

As you squeegee off the epoxy and putty you also fill the grain of the cedar as well as nearly every single staple hole and any other cavity you may have missed previously. It is a good idea to have some helpers for the entire process because *time* is important. You want everything to be done before the epoxy starts to set up. So, that means you have to roll on the sealer, apply putty to all the holes, and squeegee everything off in a relatively short time. Two people can do it if they work right along, but I recommend doing it in two parts to ensure completion of the final squeegee before the material starts to set up. With four people you can do the entire canoe. Remember there is no need to be fussy in laying down the sealer epoxy or the filler because the excess of both will soon be squeegeed off. So, it is OK to hurry through these steps, then do a thorough job with your squeegees. Anything you leave on the hull to cure will have to be sanded off before fiberglassing.

If you did a good job with those amazing squeegees you only have to sand the surface lightly by hand before applying the fiberglass cloth.

Graphite on the Canoe Bottom: I have found that Gougeon's number 423 Graphite Powder mixed with epoxy resin to be worthwhile for the bottom of my canoes. The graphite isn't necessary unless you plan to give your canoe hard use where it will be frequently called upon for whitewater or in shallow streams where it will be dragged over abrasive sand, gravel, and rocks. In this type of use the "black bottom," as we call it, does two things: the graphite acts as a lubricant to make the hull slide more easily over the obstruction; secondly, it provides a wear surface which makes it easy to see how much wear the hull has taken. If you can see the clear fiberglass, it is time to touch up your black bottom.

Gougeon recommends a mixture of 10% of graphite by volume with the epoxy, but I make a real thick mixture that is almost like tar when we roll it on. I mix until I am satisfied with the consistency, but I would say the mix is close to 40% graphite to 60% epoxy. This gives a nice thick layer. After rolling on the thick mixture the bottom will be rippled. Use a disposable foam brush to smooth it out. Be sure to mask off any areas you don't want black, because it will run.

Whitewater Kit: Through the years of hard use in my guiding business I have developed sort of a whitewater kit. Or, in automobile terms, the heavy duty package.

An important part of this package is the graphite bottom that has already been covered. The other part consists of stiffening up the bottom by the addition of more fiberglass. This is done by putting on a football-shaped piece of fiberglass on the outside and another on the inside. This really stiffens things up.

You might wonder, why not put this extra stuff on all the canoes, "just in case." Well, nothing comes for free, and the price for the increased strength is increased weight. You don't add much, but if you don't need it, why lug it around?

Finishing the Inside of the Stems: This is mostly a cosmetic tip, but it does make fiberglassing the inside of the hull easier, and besides, who doesn't want their canoe to look good? Just mix up some more of that Microlight to a nice thick putty and put a thick bead of it into the narrow vee in the bow and stern before fiberglassing. I like to use the tongue depressor-type sticks that Gougeon sells. They have a rounded end and make just the right tool for the job. Smooth it out as much as possible to minimize the amount of sanding you have to do after it has cured.

Painter Holes in the Stems: If you ever have occasion to handle your canoe with painters, or lines, in fast moving water, you know the value of having their attachment as low as possible. Instead of drilling a hole in the decks for painter attachment try making a hole in the stem a few inches above the water line.

Cut two pieces of copper tubing (I use ½″ or ¾″) two or three inches long. Next drill a hole just big enough for the tubing to pass through in the bow and stern at the desired level and about two inches back from the end. Mix epoxy with Colloidal Silica to a glue-like consistency and cover the inside of the hole and the outside of the tubing. Push the tubing in place, be sure it is well sealed, and when the epoxy mix has cured, cut off the excess tubing and sand the hull surface until it is fair. This is a strong tie-down for transport as well.

Test to Check for Glue: This was sent to me by a reader. It is always hard to be sure you have removed all the glue from the hull's surface before starting the fiberglassing process. But, if you don't get it all it will show forever. An easy way to spot the glue is to wipe the hull down with a damp cloth when you think the sanding and scraping is complete. If any pesky glue spots remain you can circle them with chalk and remove them as soon as the hull dries off.

Additional Supply Sources:

MLCS Ltd.
P.O. Box 4053 C6
Rydal, PA 19046
Tel. 1-800-533-9298
Bead and flute bits (page 34).

Tweedie Lumber
RFD#1 Box 960
Thorndike, ME 04986
Tel. (207)-568-3632
White cedar. (Will ship.)

Tom Hamilton
(See Horsepower Logging Co. listing on page 111.)
Lumber: cedar, hardwoods, and cedar strips. (Will ship.)

Catalog: Every year the folks at Gougeon Brothers come up with new and improved products. Keep a current catalog on hand to stay informed. In addition you should be sure to receive their free publication called *The Boatbuilder.* It is a great magazine and it will keep you up-to-date with boat building technology using WEST SYSTEM® products.

Appendix I

Supply Sources

Fasteners

Majestic Fasteners, Inc.
Box 193
Morris Plains, NJ 07950
Bronze and brass fastenings.

New Freedom Boat Works
Rt. 1, Box 12
North Freedom, WI 53951
Brass bolts.

Old Town Canoe Company
35 Middle St.
Old Town, ME 04468
Brass bolts.

Stiles Boat Supply
Box 11, Linden Ave.
Mantua Heights, NJ 08051
Bronze and brass fastenings.

The Wooden Boat Shop
1007 Northeast Boat St.
Seattle, WA 98105
Specialty items and fastenings. Catalog — $1.50.

Wooden Canoe Heritage Association
Box 5634
Madison, WI 53705
Brass machine bolts, brass carriage bolts, other. (Also, a good organization to join for anyone interested in wood canoes.)

William Alvarez and Co.
Box 245, 350 East Orangethorpe Ave., Unit 5
Placentia, CA 92670
Bronze and brass fastenings.

Fiberglassing supplies

W.A. Clark and Associates
Sugarloaf Star Route
Boulder, CO 80302
Polyester and epoxy resins and fiberglassing supplies, marine hardware, information.

Boatex Fiberglass Company, Inc.
Natick, MA 01760
Polyester resin, fiberglass, fiberglassing supplies.

Clark Craft Boat Co.
16 Aqua Lane
Tonawanda, NY 14150
Epoxy and polyester resins, fiberglassing supplies, also fasteners. Catalog.

Gougeon Brothers, Inc.
706 Martin St.
Bay City, MI 48706
WEST SYSTEM resins and products. Catalog.

Hamilton Marine
Searsport, ME 04974
Epoxy and polyester resins, fiberglassing supplies. Catalog.

Lumber

F. Scott Jay and Co., Inc.
P.O. Box 146, 8174 Ritchie Highway
Pasadena, MD 21122
White oak, ash, mahogany, Sitka spruce, red cedar, white cedar.

Flounder Bay Boat Lumber
3rd & "O" Streets
Anacortes, WA 98221
Hardwoods and boatbuilding supplies.

Horsepower Logging Co.
Tom Hamilton
RFD#1, Box 192
Cornville, ME 04976
Tel. (207) 474-3973
Can furnish quality cedar and hardwood, long lumber.

Jonesboro Milling Co.
Box 99
Jonesboro ME 04648
Long lumber, cedar boat lumber.

Maurice L. Condon Co., Inc.
250 Ferris Ave.
White Plains, NY 10603
Sitka spruce, mahogany, white oak, red cedar, white cedar.

Northern Michigan Boat Wood
Box 135
Lake Leelanau, MI 49653
Tel. (616) 256-9658
Sitka spruce, western red-cedar, white cedar, mahogany, teak, white oak.

Penberthy Lumber Company
5800 South Boyle Ave.
Los Angeles CA 90058
Ash, mahogany, maple, white oak, spruce.

Sprowl Brothers, Inc.
Searsmont, ME 04973
Can furnish all wood materials for a strip canoe. Inquiries invited, will furnish prices on request.

Yukon Lumber Company
520 West 22nd St.
Norfolk VA 23517
Mahogany, white ash, Sitka spruce, ash, white cedar.

Cane for Seats

The H. H. Perkins Co.
10 South Bradley Road
Woodbridge, CT 06525
Chair-caning supplies, plastic and natural.

Special Tools

Furnima Industrial Carbide
Biernackie Road, P.O. Box 308
Barry's Bay, Ontario
Canada KOJ 1BO
Tel. (613) 756-3657
Router bits for cutting beads and flutes in canoe strips.

Appendix II

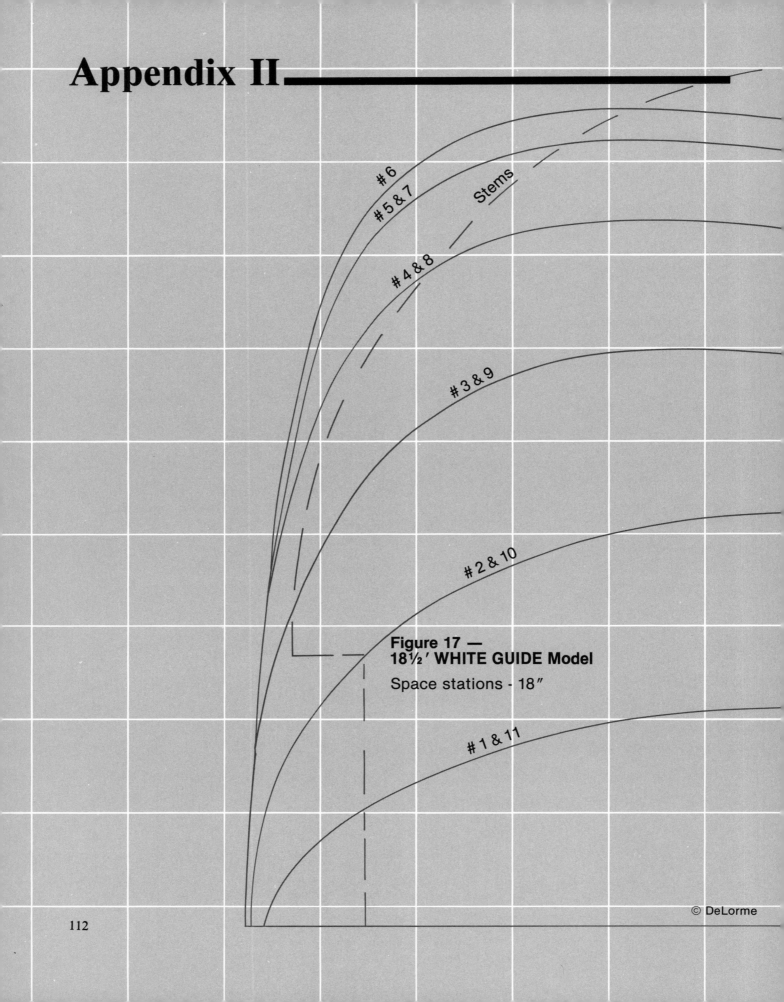

#6

#5 & 7

Stems

#4 & 8

#3 & 9

#2 & 10

**Figure 17 —
18½′ WHITE GUIDE Model**

Space stations - 18″

#1 & 11

© DeLorme

This is a half-scale pattern. In use simply enlarge the pattern **2:1**. Make your grid squares for enlargement 2″ × 2″.

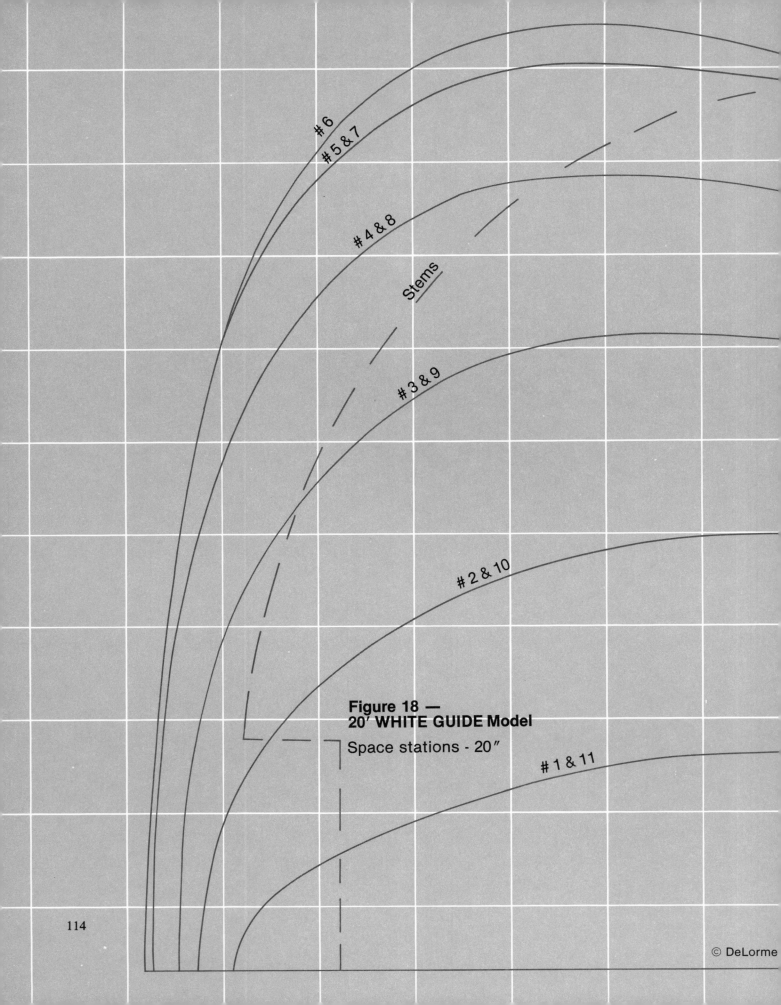

#6

#5 & 7

#4 & 8

Stems

#3 & 9

#2 & 10

**Figure 18 —
20′ WHITE GUIDE Model**

Space stations - 20″

#1 & 11

114

© DeLorme

This is a half-scale pattern. In use simply enlarge the pattern **2:1**. Make your grid squares for enlargement 2″ × 2″.

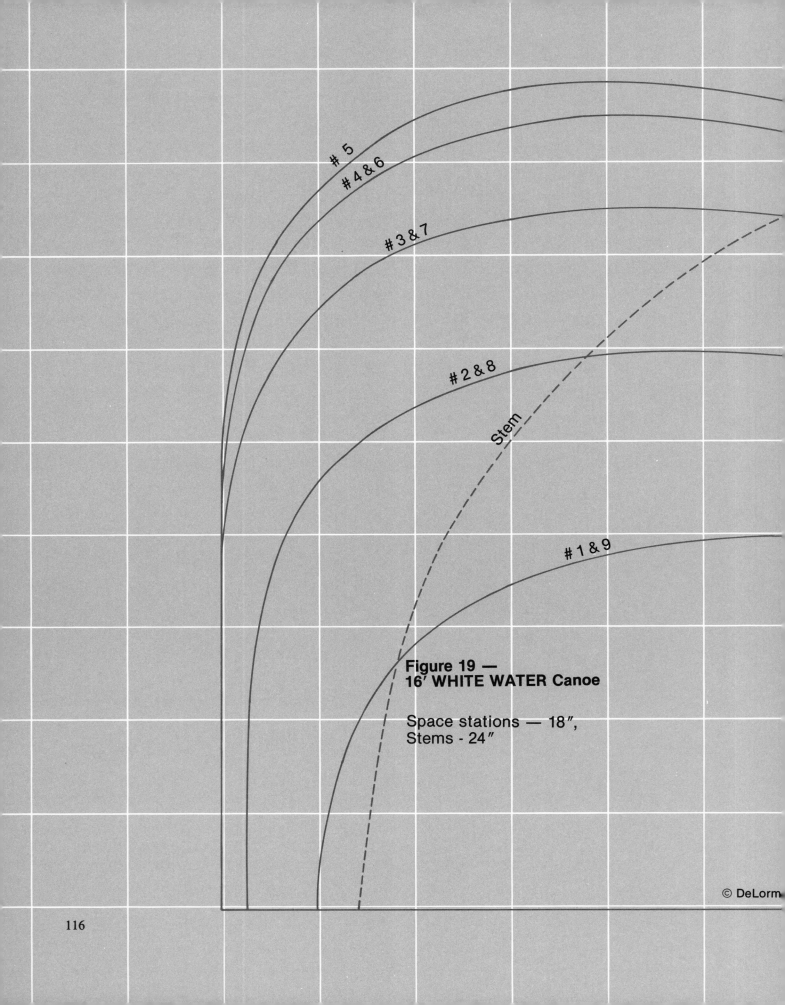

5

4 & 6

3 & 7

2 & 8

Stem

1 & 9

**Figure 19 —
16′ WHITE WATER Canoe**

Space stations — 18″,
Stems - 24″

© DeLorm

116

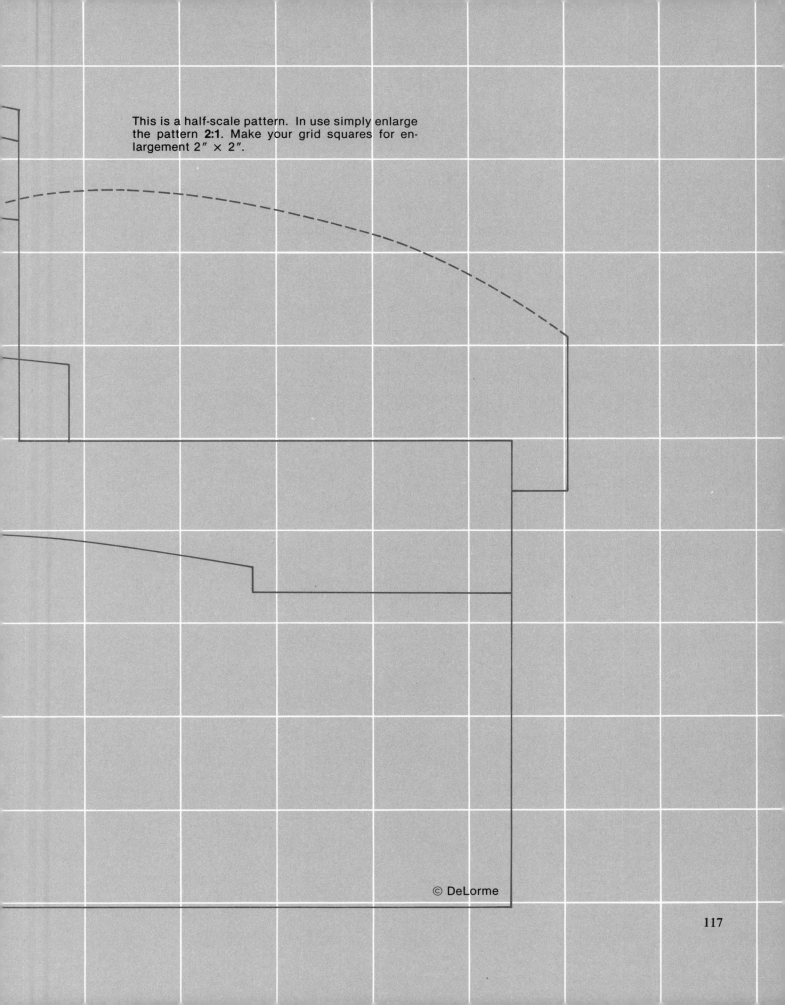

This is a half-scale pattern. In use simply enlarge the pattern **2:1**. Make your grid squares for enlargement 2″ × 2″.

© DeLorme

117

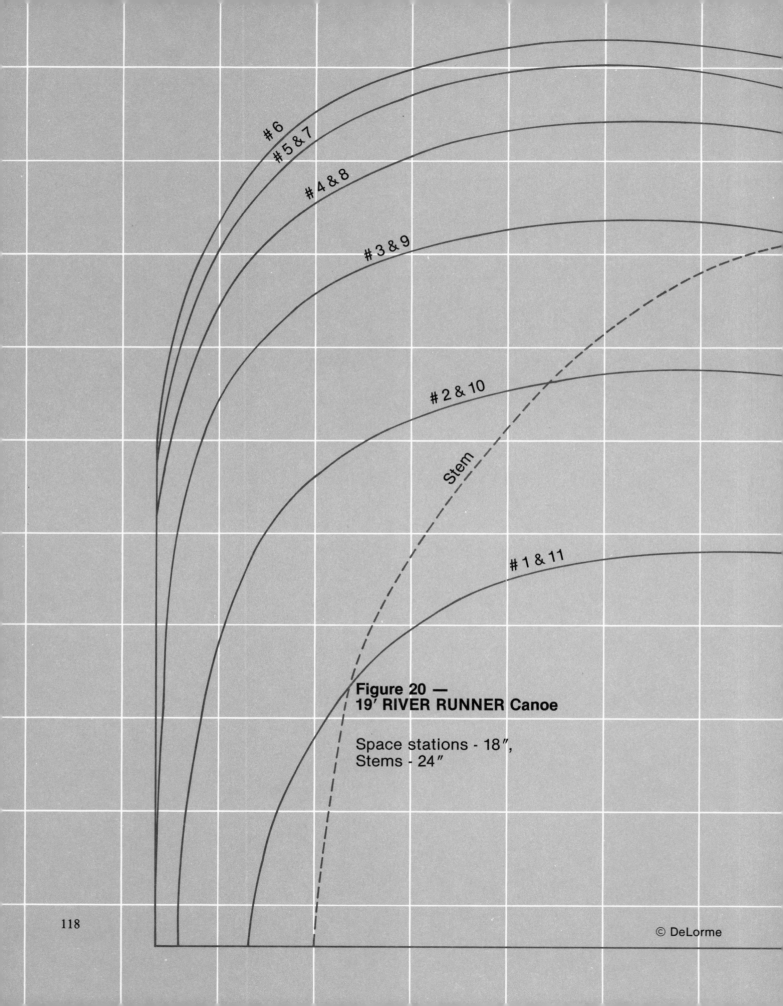

#6

#5 & 7

#4 & 8

#3 & 9

#2 & 10

Stem

#1 & 11

**Figure 20 —
19′ RIVER RUNNER Canoe**

Space stations - 18″,
Stems - 24″

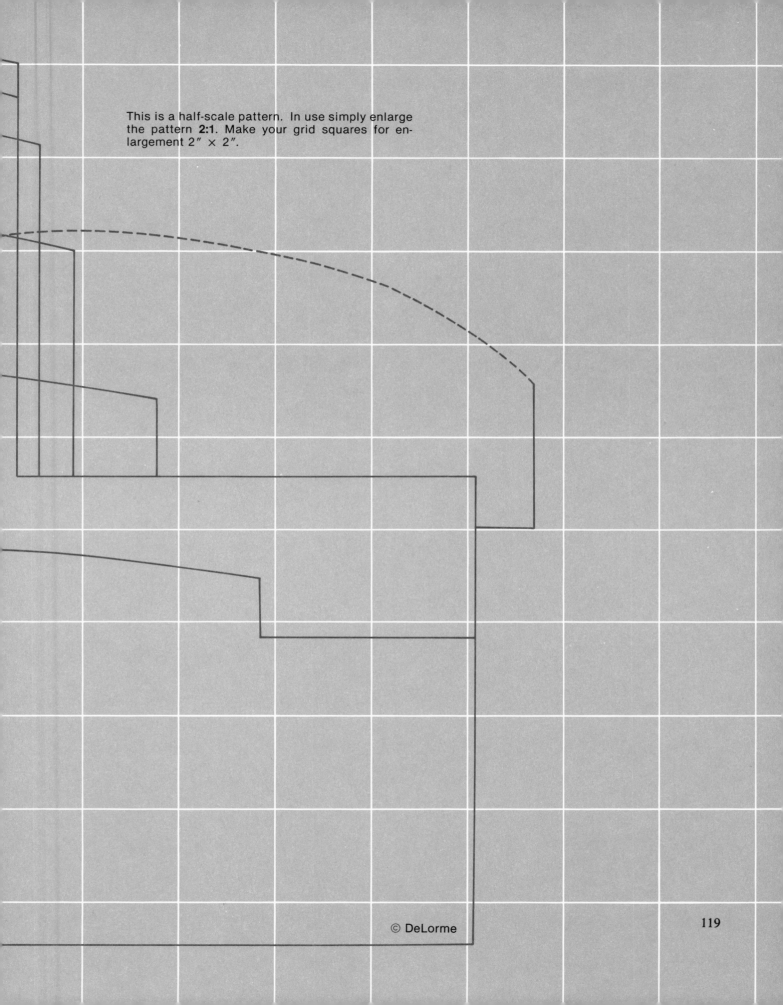

This is a half-scale pattern. In use simply enlarge the pattern **2:1**. Make your grid squares for enlargement 2″ × 2″.

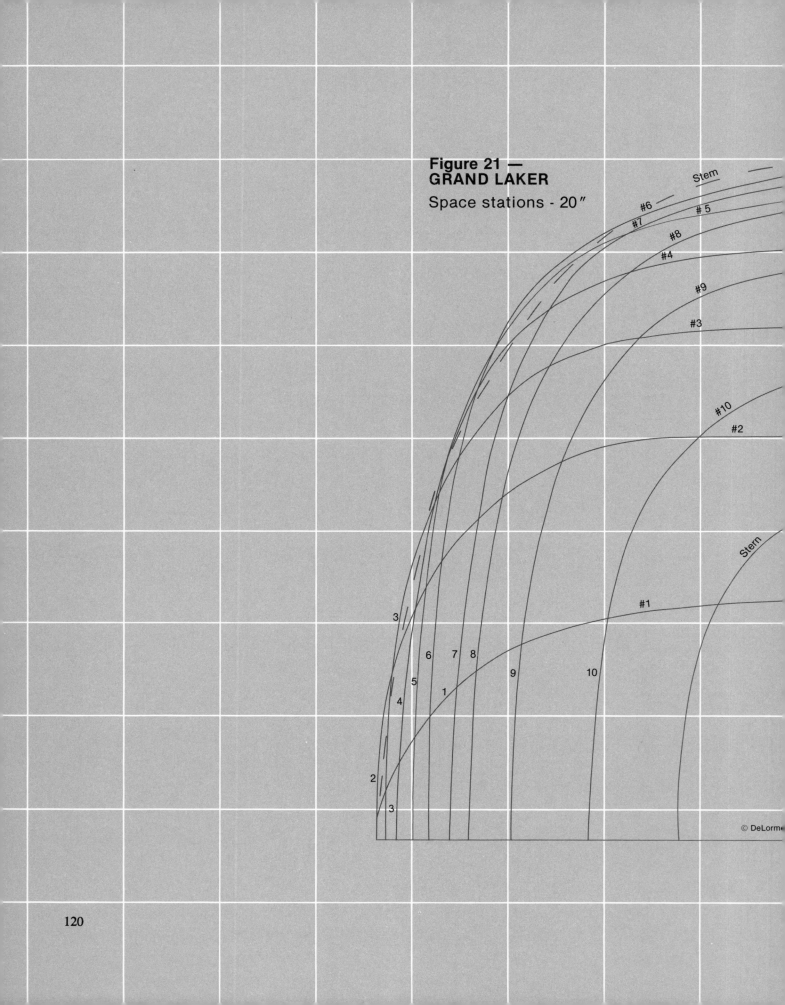

**Figure 21 —
GRAND LAKER**

Space stations - 20″

© DeLorme

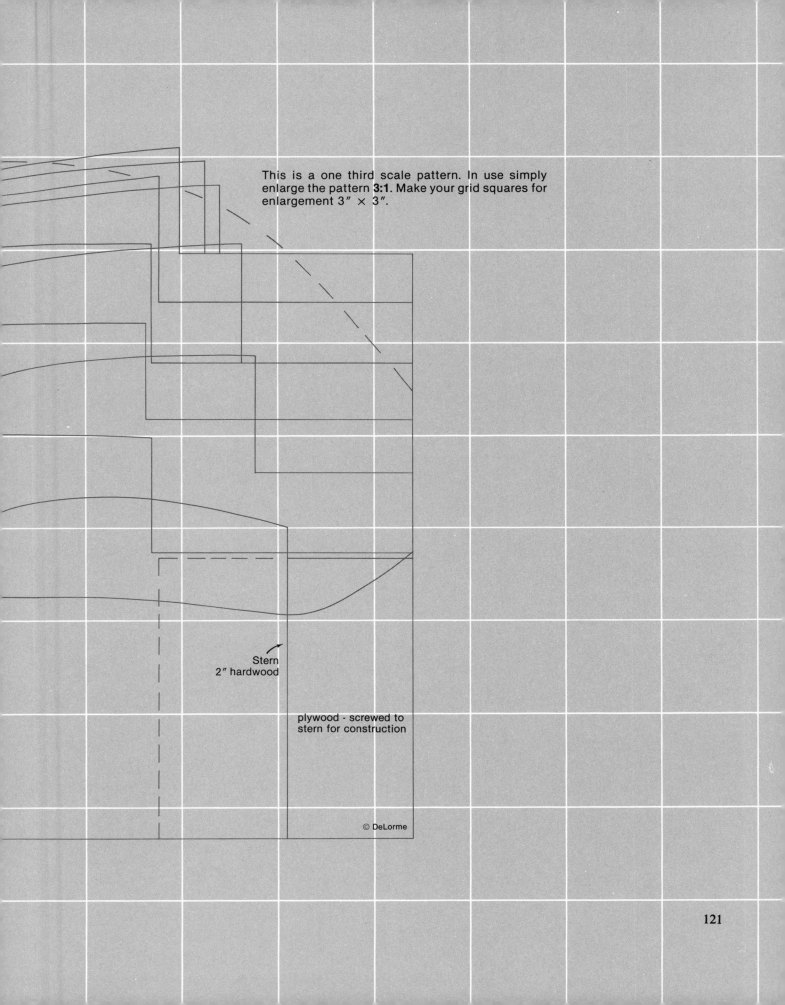

This is a one third scale pattern. In use simply enlarge the pattern **3:1**. Make your grid squares for enlargement 3″ × 3″.

Stern
2″ hardwood

plywood - screwed to
stern for construction

© DeLorme

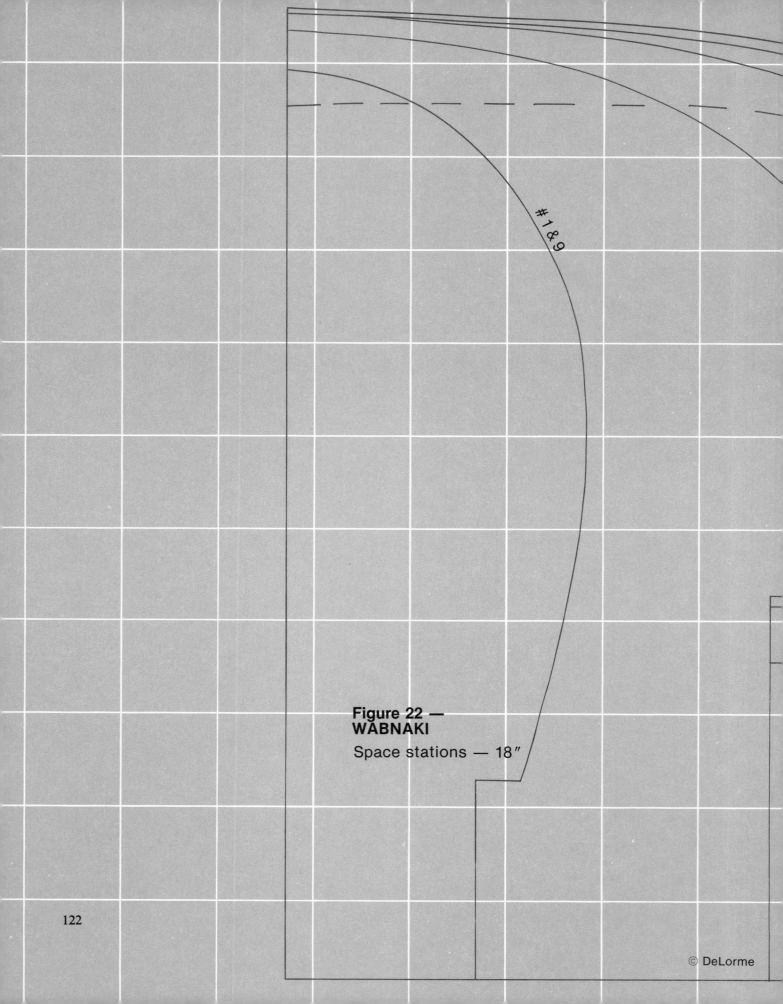

#1&9

**Figure 22 —
WABNAKI**
Space stations — 18″

#5

#4 & 6

#3 & 7

#2 & 8

This is a half-scale pattern. In use simply enlarge the pattern **2:1**. Make your grid squares for enlargement 2″ × 2″.

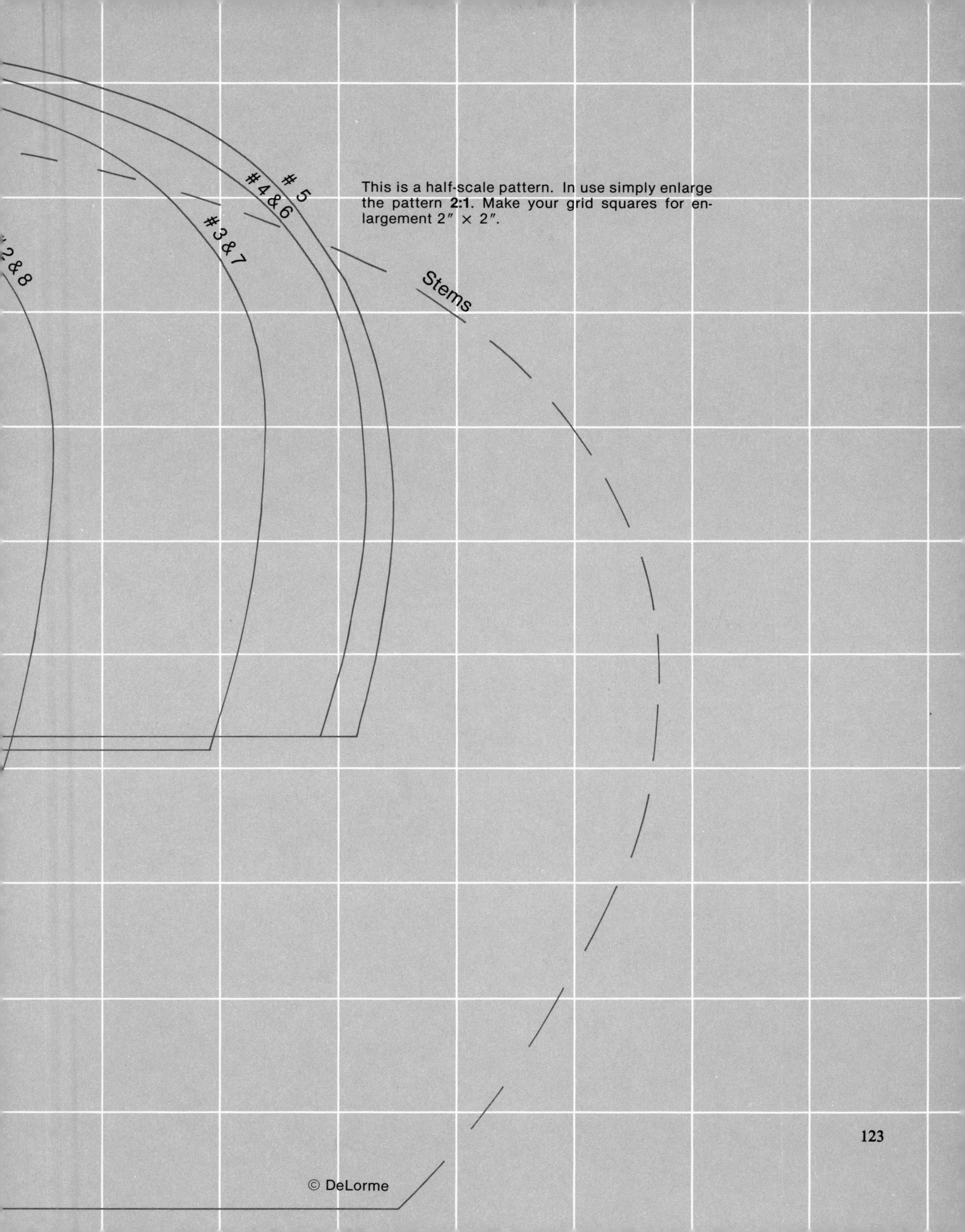

Stems

123

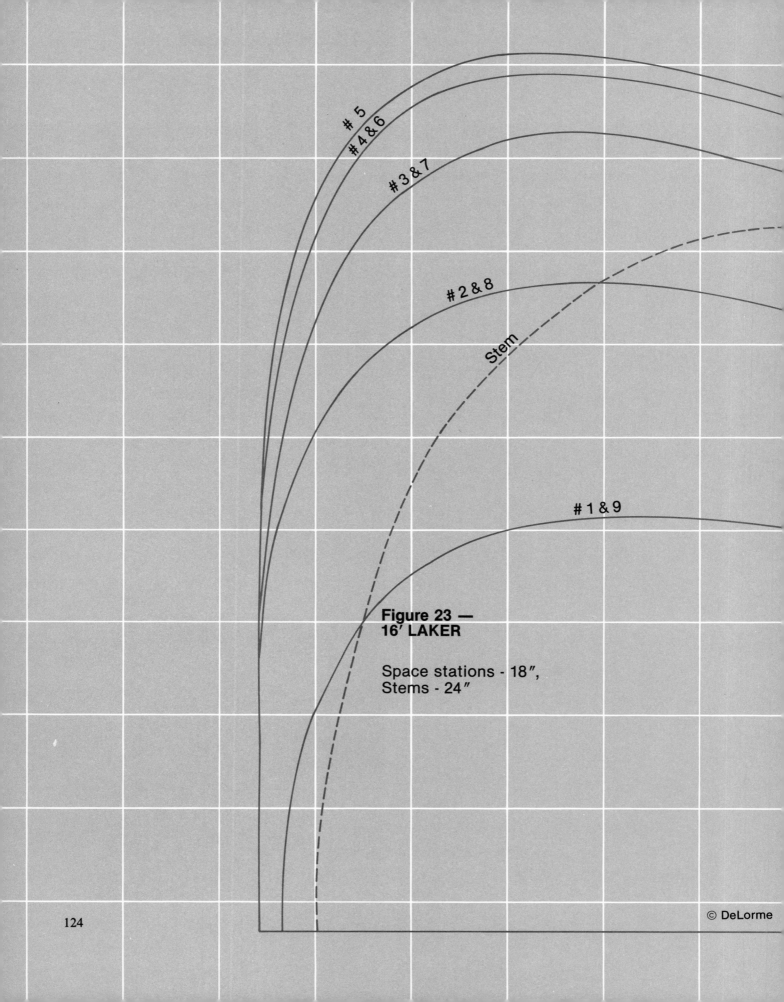

5

4 & 6

3 & 7

2 & 8

Stem

1 & 9

**Figure 23 —
16′ LAKER**

Space stations - 18″,
Stems - 24″

© DeLorme

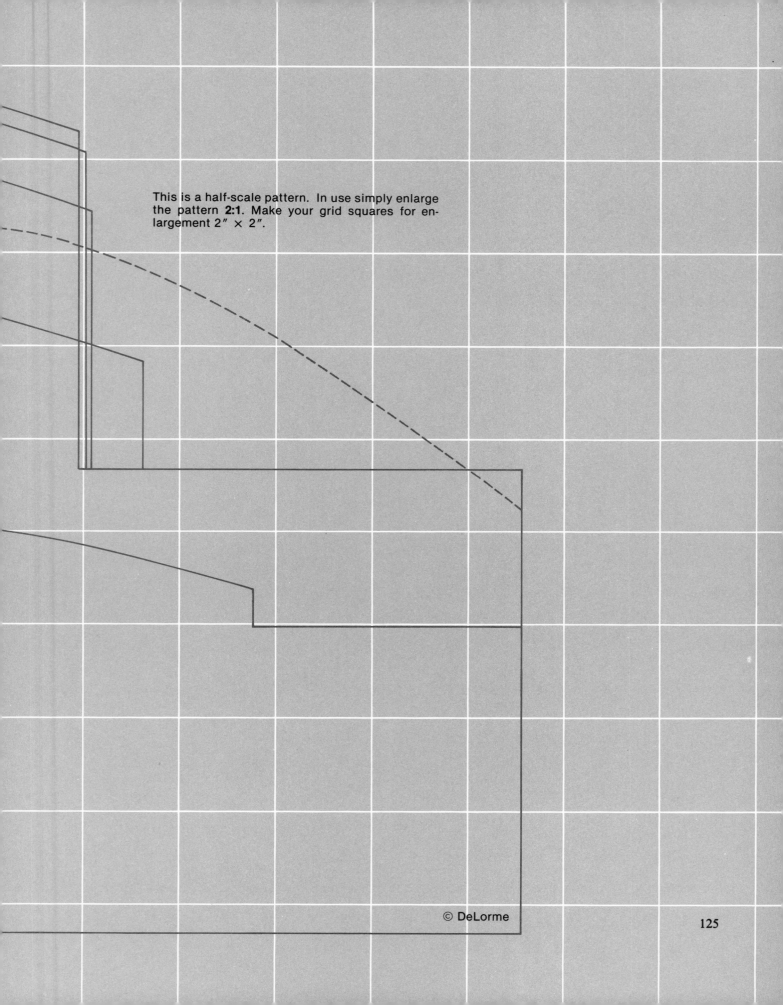

This is a half-scale pattern. In use simply enlarge the pattern **2:1**. Make your grid squares for enlargement 2″ × 2″.

125

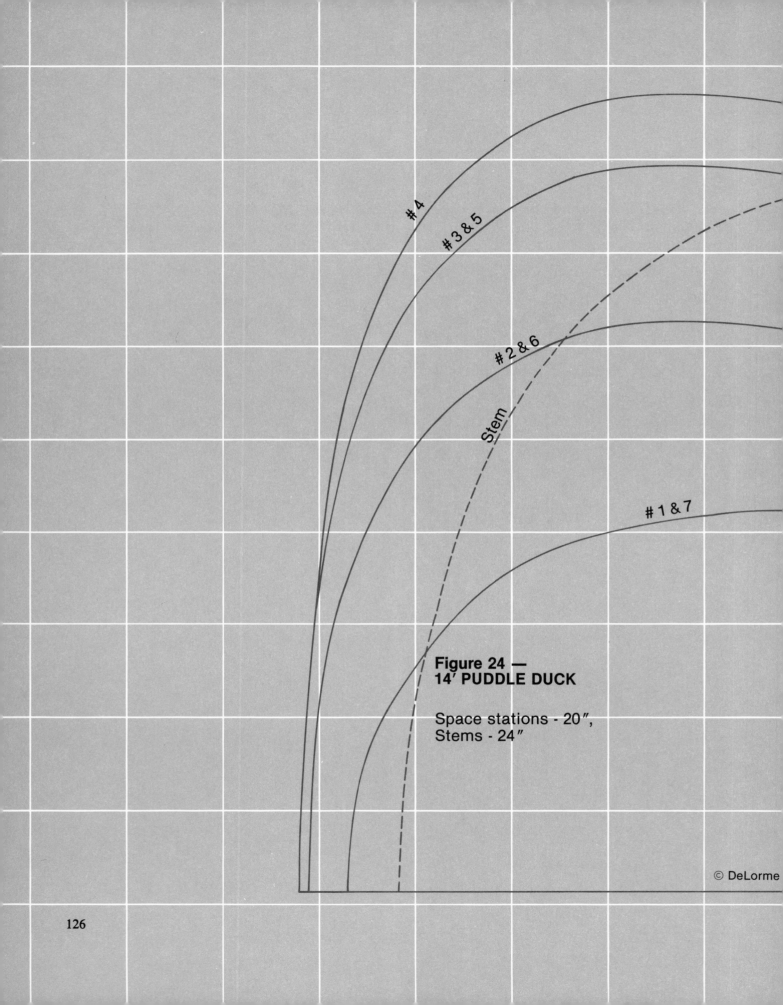

#4

#3 & 5

#2 & 6

Stem

#1 & 7

Figure 24 —
14′ PUDDLE DUCK

Space stations - 20″,
Stems - 24″

© DeLorme

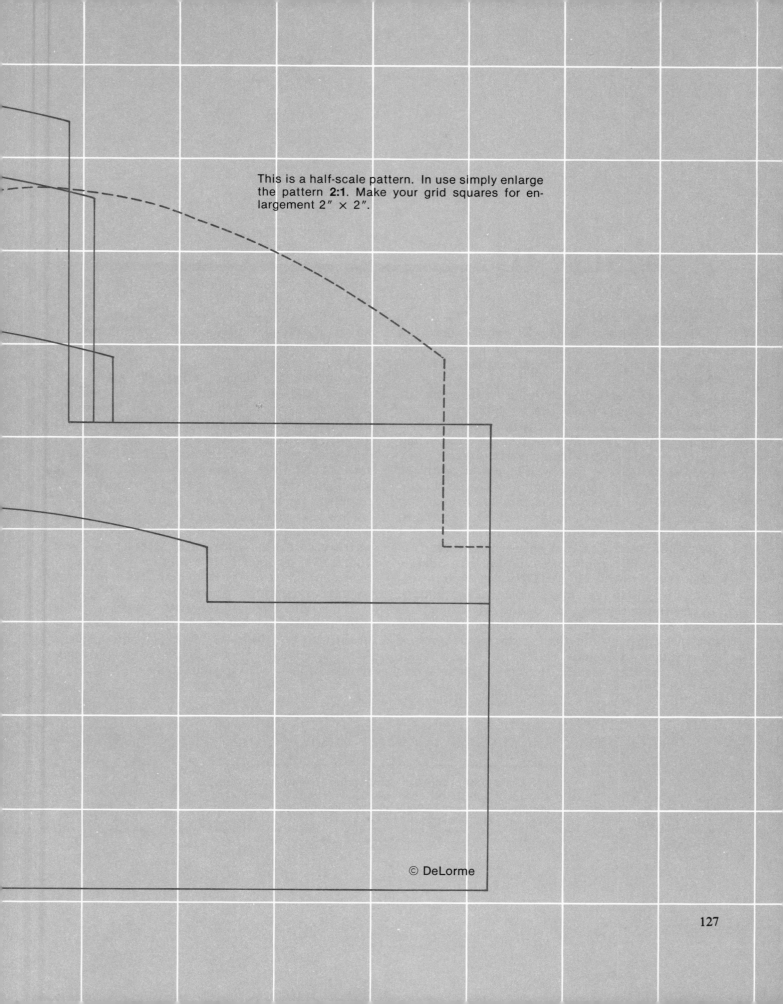

This is a half-scale pattern. In use simply enlarge the pattern **2:1**. Make your grid squares for enlargement 2″ × 2″.

© DeLorme

Appendix III

Enlarging Patterns

Enlarging patterns to full size is an easy task. If a pattern requires a 2:1 enlargement you have to convert the pattern to twice the size of what appears in the book.

The grid squares printed in this book are all one inch. On a separate sheet of large paper (at least double the size of the pattern in both directions, approximately 22″×34″) start in one corner and draw two inch squares lightly over the entire sheet. Keep them light so they won't interfere with the pattern but dark enough so you can see them. When this is done, count the number of squares to ensure that you have enough to cover the pattern. Begin to draw on a square that allows you to get the whole pattern on your enlargement sheet.

Some people experienced at pattern enlargements simply do it by eye. However the most accurate way is to take measurements. This is done by measuring the distance, on the printed pattern, from where a pattern line crosses the grid, doubling the measurement and finding this point on your enlargement. Continue to do this for a single square and then connect the dots. This is a sure way of maintaining perspective of where the pattern lines should be relative to the edges of each square.

After you've enlarged the pattern on the first three or four squares, check to be sure that you are getting the same shape that appears on the printed pattern. If yours looks different check to see if you doubled the distance when you transferred it to your enlargement. If this is not the case then make sure that you are accurately drawing or curving your lines in the corresponding position with respect to the edges of each square.

Now that you are on the right track continue with each section of the pattern until you've completed each station. Remember, the stations give your canoe its shape. Take care in your enlargements and when you're ready to use your patterns to make the stations, be accurate.

These same directions apply to a pattern that is printed one-third actual size (3:1 enlargement necessary). Simply make three inch squares on a sheet big enough to accomodate the enlarged pattern and follow the same directions.

For a blueprint of full size plans for any one of the models shown in this book send $20.00 with model name and length to: DeLorme Publishing Company, P.O. Box 298, Freeport, Maine 04032